WILLIAMS-SONOMA

ICE CREAM

RECIPES AND TEXT
MARY GOODBODY

GENERAL EDITOR
CHUCK WILLIAMS

PHOTOGRAPHS
NOEL BARNHURST

SIMON & SCHUSTER • **SOURCE**

NEW YORK • LONDON • TORONTO • SYDNEY • SINGAPORE

CONTENTS

ELEGANT ICE CREAMS

INDULGENT ICE CREAMS

ICE CREAM DISHES

INTRODUCTION

The best ice creams are really just combinations of a few essential ingredients: cream, whole milk, eggs, and sugar, mixed with delicious flavorings such as fresh fruit, fine chocolate, and nuts. And, the freshly made ice creams you make at home from these simple ingredients will far surpass anything you can find in a store. Years ago, making homemade ice cream meant having to use a large hand-cranked machine that required an abundance of crushed ice and rock salt. Thankfully, the electric machines of today have made the process much simpler. In a matter of minutes, you can create delicious, homemade ice cream, gelato, or sorbet.

Page through the recipes in this book to find your favorite flavors as well as fresh new ideas. The detailed side notes that accompany each recipe and informative basics section teach you all you need to know to make some of the most delicious ice creams you have ever tasted. Once you have sampled some of the flavors inside, you will quickly realize that homemade ice cream is simply the best there is!

Chuck Williams

THE CLASSICS

Vanilla or chocolate? When it comes to choosing a flavor of ice cream, this is the age-old dilemma. But vanilla and chocolate are just two of the flavors that will never go out of fashion. Likewise, coffee, strawberry, and mint–chocolate chip deserve places of honor. Add orange sherbet and lemon sorbet, and you have a short list of irresistible classics.

VANILLA BEAN ICE CREAM
10

DOUBLE-CHOCOLATE ICE CREAM
13

COFFEE ICE CREAM
14

STRAWBERRY ICE CREAM
17

MINT–CHOCOLATE CHIP ICE CREAM
18

ORANGE SHERBET
21

MEYER LEMON SORBET
22

VANILLA BEAN ICE CREAM

In a heavy 2-qt (2-l) saucepan, combine the milk and 1 cup (8 fl oz / 250 ml) of the cream. Using the tip of a sharp knife, scrape the seeds from the vanilla bean into the milk mixture and then add the vanilla bean. Cook over medium heat until bubbles form around the edges of the pan, about 5 minutes.

Meanwhile, combine the egg yolks, sugar, and remaining ½ cup (4 fl oz / 125 ml) cream in a bowl. Whisk until the mixture is smooth and the sugar begins to dissolve.

Remove the milk mixture from the heat. Gradually whisk about ½ cup (4 fl oz / 125 ml) of the hot milk mixture into the egg mixture, whisking constantly, until smooth. Pour the egg mixture into the saucepan. Cook over medium heat, stirring constantly with a wooden spoon and keeping the custard at a low simmer, until it is thick enough to coat the back of the spoon and leaves a clear trail when a finger is drawn through it, 4–6 minutes. Do not let the custard boil. Strain through a fine-mesh sieve into a bowl. Discard the vanilla bean.

Place the bowl in a larger bowl partially filled with ice cubes and water. Stir occasionally until cool. Cover with plastic wrap, pressing it directly on the surface of the custard to prevent a skin from forming. Refrigerate until chilled, at least 3 hours or up to 24 hours.

Pour the custard into an ice-cream maker and freeze according to the manufacturer's instructions. Transfer the ice cream to a freezer-safe container. Cover and freeze until firm, at least 3 hours or up to 3 days, before serving.

MAKES ABOUT 1 QUART (32 FL OZ / 1 L)

1½ cups (12 fl oz / 375 ml) whole milk

1½ cups (12 fl oz / 375 ml) heavy (double) cream

1 vanilla bean, split lengthwise

6 large egg yolks

½ cup (4 oz / 125 g) plus 2 tablespoons sugar

VANILLA BEANS

The primary types of vanilla beans available are Bourbon-Madagascar, Tahitian, and Mexican. Bourbon-Madagascar beans, the most common, have a stronger flavor than the more floral Tahitian beans. Mexican beans carry the boldest flavor of the three. Some Mexican beans contain coumarin, however, a substance that can be toxic, so purchase them only from a reputable source. If you are unable to find vanilla beans, use pure vanilla extract (essence). The addition of 1½ teaspoons of extract delivers a flavor punch about equal to that of the seeds from a single bean.

DOUBLE-CHOCOLATE ICE CREAM

1½ cups (12 fl oz/375 ml) whole milk

1½ cups (12 fl oz/375 ml) heavy (double) cream

4 large egg yolks

½ cup (4 oz/125 g) sugar

2 tablespoons unsweetened nonalkalized cocoa powder (page 114)

Pinch of salt

6 oz (185 g) bittersweet or semisweet (plain) chocolate, coarsely chopped

2 teaspoons vanilla extract (essence)

In a heavy 2-qt (2-l) saucepan, combine the milk and 1 cup (8 fl oz/250 ml) of the cream. Cook over medium heat until bubbles form around the edges of the pan, about 5 minutes.

Meanwhile, combine the egg yolks, sugar, cocoa, salt, and remaining ½ cup (4 fl oz/125 ml) cream in a bowl. Whisk until the mixture is smooth and the sugar begins to dissolve.

Remove the milk mixture from the heat. Gradually whisk about ½ cup (4 fl oz/125 ml) of the hot milk mixture into the egg mixture, whisking constantly, until smooth. Pour the egg mixture into the saucepan. Cook over medium heat, stirring constantly with a wooden spoon and keeping the custard at a low simmer, until it is thick enough to coat the back of the spoon and leaves a clear trail when a finger is drawn through it, 4–6 minutes. Do not let the custard boil. Put the chocolate in a heatproof bowl and pour the hot custard over it. Stir until the chocolate melts and the custard is smooth. Strain the custard through a fine-mesh sieve into a bowl. Add the vanilla and stir to combine.

Place the bowl in a larger bowl partially filled with ice cubes and water. Stir occasionally until cool. Cover with plastic wrap, pressing it directly on the surface of the custard to prevent a skin from forming. Refrigerate until chilled, at least 3 hours or up to 24 hours.

Pour the custard into an ice-cream maker and freeze according to the manufacturer's instructions. Transfer the ice cream to a freezer-safe container. Cover and freeze until firm, at least 3 hours or up to 3 days, before serving.

Serving Tip: Chocolate curls can be a pretty garnish for this ice cream. To make curls, wrap a piece of chocolate in plastic wrap and rub between your hands for 1–2 minutes to warm it up. Unwrap and use a vegetable peeler to slowly and evenly scrape the chocolate into curls.

MAKES ABOUT 1 QUART (32 FL OZ/1 L)

CHOCOLATE VARIETIES

Different varieties of chocolate are defined by how much chocolate liquor they contain, which also determines the depth of their chocolate flavor. Bittersweet and semisweet usually contain nearly the same amount of chocolate liquor along with cocoa butter and sugar, thus either type can be used in this recipe. Semisweet is typically slightly sweeter, however. But not all chocolate varieties are interchangeable. For this recipe, do not use unsweetened or baking chocolate, which is 100 percent liquor, or milk chocolate, which contains at least 12 percent milk solids.

COFFEE ICE CREAM

In a bowl, mix the milk, cream, and brewed coffee together.

In a separate bowl, combine the sugar and salt. Add the milk mixture and whisk until the sugar dissolves. Add the vanilla and stir to combine. Set aside, stirring occasionally, to allow the flavors to blend, about 15 minutes.

Cover and refrigerate the mixture until chilled, at least 3 hours or up to 8 hours.

Pour the mixture into an ice-cream maker and freeze according to the manufacturer's instructions. Transfer the ice cream to a freezer-safe container. Cover and freeze until firm, at least 3 hours or up to 3 days, before serving.

MAKES ABOUT 1 QUART (32 FL OZ/1 L)

1½ cups (12 fl oz/375 ml) whole milk

1½ cups (12 fl oz/375 ml) heavy (double) cream

1 cup (8 fl oz/250 ml) brewed dark-roast coffee, chilled

½ cup (4 oz/125 g) plus 1 tablespoon sugar

Pinch of salt

1 teaspoon vanilla extract (essence)

COFFEE VARIETIES

Coffee beans are roasted to bring out their rich flavor, and the roasting method determines the final flavor of the brewed cup. Dark-roasted beans produce dark, rich coffee, such as that brewed from French and Italian roast beans. These beans make inky, full-bodied coffee, including espresso. To give this ice cream a full coffee flavor, use freshly ground, dark-roasted beans. The ice cream will not have the same intensity if made with medium-roast beans or with instant coffee or espresso powder—but it will still taste delicious.

STRAWBERRY ICE CREAM

2 cups (16 fl oz/500 ml) heavy (double) cream

1 cup (8 fl oz/250 ml) whole milk

¾ cup (6 oz/185 g) sugar

Pinch of salt

1 teaspoon vanilla extract (essence)

2 cups (8 oz/250 g) fresh strawberries, stemmed and coarsely chopped, plus extra for optional garnish

In a bowl, combine the cream and milk. Add the sugar and salt and whisk until the sugar begins to dissolve. Stir in the vanilla. Set aside, stirring occasionally, to allow the flavors to blend, about 15 minutes.

Cover and refrigerate the mixture until chilled, at least 3 hours or up to 8 hours.

In a bowl, using a fork or potato masher, mash half of the chopped strawberries; they should break down into small chunks. Add the remaining coarsely chopped strawberries to the bowl. Cover and refrigerate the strawberries for about 1 hour.

Pour the milk mixture into an ice-cream maker and freeze according to the manufacturer's instructions. When nearly frozen and the consistency of thick whipped cream, add the strawberries. Churn or stir until just blended. Transfer the ice cream to a freezer-safe container. Cover and freeze until firm, at least 3 hours or up to 3 days, before serving. If desired, garnish with additional chopped strawberries before serving.

MAKES ABOUT 1½ QUARTS (48 FL OZ/1.5 L)

STRAWBERRIES
Fragrant, bright red strawberries are at their peak in spring and early summer. For the best flavor, buy small, organically grown berries from farmers' markets. They should be sweetly aromatic and vibrantly colored, and have moist green leaves and stems. Avoid berries with white or green shoulders and wilted leaves. Hull strawberries by cutting out the stem end with a small, sharp knife. For this classic ice cream, some of the berries are mashed, and the remainder is left coarsely chopped. Larger chunks of berries will turn too hard when frozen.

MINT-CHOCOLATE CHIP ICE CREAM

MELTING CHOCOLATE

The preferred way to melt chocolate is in the top pan of a double boiler (page 114) set over, but not touching, barely simmering water. As soon as the water simmers, it produces steam, the nemesis of melting chocolate. If even a droplet of moisture gets into the chocolate, it can seize or stiffen. If this happens, start over with new chocolate. Mixing the melted chocolate with vegetable oil causes the formation of small slivers of chocolate in the finished ice cream. This method, perfected by noted cookbook author Nick Malgieri, yields a distinctive and well-blended ice cream.

In a heavy 2-qt (2-l) saucepan, combine the milk, 1 cup (8 fl oz/250 ml) of the cream, and the mint leaves. Cook over medium heat until bubbles form around the edges of the pan, about 5 minutes. Remove from the heat and let stand for 20 minutes to steep.

Meanwhile, combine the egg yolks, sugar, salt, and remaining ½ cup (4 fl oz/125 ml) cream in a bowl. Whisk until smooth. Gradually whisk about ½ cup (4 fl oz/125 ml) of the warm milk mixture into the egg mixture until smooth. Pour the egg mixture into the pan. Cook over medium heat, stirring constantly with a wooden spoon and keeping the custard at a low simmer, until it is thick enough to coat the back of the spoon and leaves a clear trail when a finger is drawn through it, 4–6 minutes. Do not let the custard boil. Strain through a fine-mesh sieve into a bowl, pressing on the mint with the back of the spoon. Stir in the food colorings, if using.

Place the bowl in a larger bowl partially filled with ice cubes and water. Stir occasionally until cool. Cover with plastic wrap, pressing it directly on the surface of the custard to prevent a skin from forming. Refrigerate until chilled, at least 3 hours or up to 24 hours.

About 1 hour before freezing the ice cream, melt the chocolate in the top of a double boiler over barely simmering water *(left)*. Stir the chocolate until it is melted, then stir in the oil. Transfer to a small pitcher. Let cool to room temperature.

Pour the custard into an ice-cream maker and freeze according to the manufacturer's instructions. When nearly frozen and the consistency of thick whipped cream, add the chocolate while the machine is churning or stop the machine temporarily, add the chocolate, and restart to mix. Transfer the ice cream to a freezer-safe container. Cover and freeze until firm, at least 3 hours or up to 3 days, before serving.

MAKES ABOUT 1 QUART (32 FL OZ/1 L)

1½ cups (12 fl oz/375 ml) whole milk

1½ cups (12 fl oz/375 ml) heavy (double) cream

1 cup (1 oz/30 g) packed fresh mint leaves

4 large egg yolks

½ cup (4 oz/125 g) plus 2 tablespoons sugar

Pinch of salt

1 or 2 drops green food coloring (optional)

1 or 2 drops blue food coloring (optional)

3 oz (90 g) bittersweet or semisweet (plain) chocolate, finely chopped

2 teaspoons canola oil

ORANGE SHERBET

2 cups (16 fl oz/500 ml) fresh orange juice (from 4–6 oranges)

¼ cup (2 oz/60 g) sugar

1 cup (8 fl oz/250 ml) whole milk

In a bowl, stir the orange juice and sugar together until the sugar dissolves. Strain the mixture through a fine-mesh sieve into a nonaluminum bowl. Pour the milk into another bowl. Cover both bowls and refrigerate until chilled, at least 3 hours or up to 8 hours.

Mix the orange juice and milk together. Pour into an ice-cream maker and freeze according to the manufacturer's instructions. Transfer the sherbet to a freezer-safe container. Cover and freeze until firm, at least 3 hours or up to 3 days, before serving.

MAKES ABOUT 1 QUART (32 FL OZ/1 L)

JUICING CITRUS
Thin-skinned oranges that are heavy for their size yield the most juice. Halve them crosswise and then extract the juice with a fluted citrus juicer or a handheld reamer. You can also use a countertop mechanical press or an electric citrus juicer. Before juicing the oranges, remove any seeds from the fruit with the tip of a sharp knife.

MEYER LEMON SORBET

MEYER LEMONS
A hybrid developed by Frank Meyer in 1908, Meyer lemons are smaller, rounder, sweeter, and more fragrant than ordinary lemons. While their origin is disputed, most likely they are a cross between a lemon and a mandarin orange, which explains their relatively dark skin. Look for them in your local markets from November to May. Whether using a Meyer lemon or another variety, the full-flavored, volatile oils are in the colorful part of the peel, called the zest. For this recipe, the zest can be removed with the fine holes of a handheld grater. It is easier to zest any citrus fruit before juicing.

In a small, heavy saucepan, combine the water and sugar. Bring to a boil over medium-high heat and cook, stirring occasionally, until the sugar dissolves and the syrup is clear, about 1 minute.

Remove the syrup from the heat, add the lemon zest, and set aside to steep for about 20 minutes. Cover and refrigerate until chilled, 2–3 hours.

Add the lemon juice to the syrup and stir to combine. Pour into an ice-cream maker and freeze according to the manufacturer's instructions. Transfer the sorbet to a freezer-safe container. Cover and freeze the sorbet until firm, at least 3 hours or up to 3 days, before serving.

Note: If you do not have Meyer lemons, replace the Meyer lemon juice and zest with regular lemon juice and zest (you will need 5 or 6 large lemons). Because ordinary lemons are tarter than Meyer, you will most likely need to increase the sugar by 3–4 tablespoons.

MAKES ABOUT 1½ PINTS (24 FL OZ/750 ML)

1¼ cups (10 fl oz/310 ml) water

1 cup (8 oz/250 g) sugar

1 heaping tablespoon grated Meyer lemon zest

1½ cups (12 fl oz/375 ml) Meyer lemon juice (from about 12 Meyer lemons), chilled

FRESH FRUIT FLAVORS

Adults and children alike look forward to fresh fruits in season. Juicy, sweet, and boldly flavored, berries, melons, and tropical fruits can be made into delicious ice creams, granitas, and sorbets. Whether you crave old-time peach ice cream or a more modern mango sorbet, almost any fresh, ripe fruit can be transformed into a superb frozen confection.

BING CHERRY ICE CREAM
26

COUNTRY PEACH ICE CREAM
29

HONEYDEW MELON GRANITA
30

BLACKBERRY SORBET
33

MANGO SORBET
34

CRANBERRY SORBET
37

AVOCADO ICE CREAM
38

BING CHERRY ICE CREAM

In a small saucepan, combine the water, ¾ cup (6 oz/185 g) of the sugar, and the cherries. Bring to a boil over medium heat, stirring occasionally, until the sugar dissolves. Remove from the heat and let the cherries steep for 30 minutes. Drain the cherries and discard the syrup. Transfer the cherries to a bowl, cover, and refrigerate for at least 30 minutes or up to 8 hours.

In a food processor, process the cream cheese until smooth, about 30 seconds. Scrape down the sides of the bowl.

Meanwhile, combine the milk, cream, and remaining ¾ cup (6 oz/185 g) sugar in a saucepan. Cook over medium heat, stirring occasionally to help dissolve the sugar, until bubbles form around the edges of the pan, about 5 minutes.

Add about ½ cup (4 fl oz/125 ml) of the hot milk mixture to the cream cheese and process until smooth, about 30 seconds. Add the remaining milk mixture and process for another 30 seconds. Strain through a fine-mesh sieve into a bowl. Add the vanilla and stir to combine. Cover and refrigerate until chilled, at least 3 hours or up to 24 hours.

Pour the cream mixture into an ice-cream maker and freeze according to the manufacturer's instructions. When nearly frozen and the consistency of thick whipped cream, add the cherries. Churn or stir just until mixed. Transfer the ice cream to a freezer-safe container. Cover and freeze until firm, at least 3 hours or up to 3 days, before serving.

Note: For the right consistency in this ice cream, use commercial cream cheese, such as Philadelphia brand, not natural or low-fat cream cheese.

MAKES ABOUT 1 QUART (32 FL OZ/1 L)

½ cup (4 fl oz/125 ml) water

1½ cups (12 oz/370 g) sugar

2 cups (16 oz/500 g) fresh Bing cherries, stemmed, pitted, and halved

6 oz (185 g) cream cheese, at room temperature (see Note)

1½ cups (12 fl oz/375 ml) whole milk

1 cup (8 fl oz/250 ml) heavy (double) cream

1 teaspoon vanilla extract (essence)

BING CHERRIES

Fresh cherries are an early summer treat. Dark red Bing cherries, the most common variety, are sold loose with their stems attached. Choose large, plump, smooth, dark fruits—the darker the cherry, the sweeter the flavor. Avoid any that are rock hard; once picked, cherries do not ripen further. Other common sweet cherries include the Lambert and the Royal Ann, but Bings are best for ice cream. Remove the pits with a small, sharp knife or use a cherry pitter, a small, efficient, specially designed hand tool.

COUNTRY PEACH ICE CREAM

4 large, ripe peaches, peeled *(far right),* then halved, pitted, and chopped into small chunks

1½ tablespoons fresh lemon juice (from about ½ lemon)

½ cup (4 oz/125 g) sugar, plus 2 tablespoons

1½ cups (12 fl oz/375 ml) whole milk

1½ cups (12 fl oz/375 ml) heavy (double) cream

4 large egg yolks

Pinch of salt

1 teaspoon vanilla extract (essence)

Put half the peaches in a bowl, and mash slightly with a fork. Sprinkle with the lemon juice and the 2 tablespoons sugar and toss to combine. Cover and refrigerate.

In a heavy 2-qt (2-l) saucepan, combine the milk, 1 cup (8 fl oz/250 ml) of the cream, and the remaining peaches. Cook over medium heat until slightly thickened, 4–5 minutes. Do not let boil. Strain through a fine-mesh sieve into a bowl, pressing on the peaches with the back of a spoon. Discard the solids.

Meanwhile, combine the egg yolks, ½ cup (4 oz/125 g) sugar, salt, and remaining ½ cup (4 fl oz/125 ml) cream in a bowl. Whisk until the mixture is smooth and the sugar begins to dissolve.

Gradually whisk about ½ cup (4 fl oz/125 ml) of the warm milk mixture into the egg mixture until smooth. Pour the egg and milk mixtures into the saucepan. Cook over medium heat, stirring constantly with a wooden spoon and keeping the custard at a low simmer, until it is thick enough to coat the back of the spoon and leaves a clear trail when a finger is drawn through it, 4–6 minutes. Do not let the custard boil. Strain through a fine-mesh sieve into a bowl. Add the vanilla and stir to combine.

Place the bowl in a larger bowl partially filled with ice cubes and water. Stir occasionally until cool. Cover with plastic wrap, pressing it directly on the surface of the custard to prevent a skin from forming. Refrigerate until chilled, at least 3 hours or up to 24 hours.

Pour the custard into an ice-cream maker and freeze according to the manufacturer's instructions. When nearly frozen and the consistency of thick whipped cream, add the reserved peaches. Churn or stir just until mixed. Transfer the ice cream to a freezer-safe container. Cover and freeze until firm, at least 6 hours or up to 3 days, before serving.

MAKES ABOUT 1 QUART (32 FL OZ/1 L)

PEELING PEACHES

It is easy to peel the thin, fuzzy skins from peaches if you blanch them first. Fill a large saucepan with water and bring to a boil. Cut a shallow X on the blossom end of each peach. One by one, carefully slip the peaches into the boiling water and blanch for 30–45 seconds. With a slotted spoon, lift the peaches from the water and set aside until cool to the touch. Using your fingertips or a small, sharp knife, slip off the skins. This method also works for peeling apricots and plums.

HONEYDEW MELON GRANITA

In a small, heavy saucepan, combine the water and sugar. Bring to a boil over medium-high heat and cook, stirring occasionally, until the sugar dissolves and the syrup is clear, about 1 minute. Set aside and let cool to room temperature.

Scoop the melon flesh into a food processor and purée just until the melon is smooth, about 20 seconds.

Cut a piece of cheesecloth (muslin) 24–26 inches (60–66 cm) long, rinse in cold water, wring out, and lay it in a colander 10–12 inches (25–30 cm) in diameter. Set the colander over a bowl. (The cheesecloth will overlap the colander by several inches; dampening it prevents it from absorbing the melon juice). Transfer the puréed melon to the colander and let drain, about 10 minutes. Lift the cheesecloth and twist the ends together tightly to squeeze out all the excess juice. Discard the pulp.

Stir about 6 tablespoons (3 fl oz/90 ml) of the sugar syrup, 3 tablespoons lime juice, and the salt into the melon juice. Taste and add more syrup or lime juice, if necessary. Cover and refrigerate until chilled, at least 2 hours or up to 8 hours.

Pour the mixture into a shallow pan, ideally a 9-by-13-inch (23-by-33-cm) jelly-roll pan. Cover with aluminum foil and freeze until the mixture begins to harden around the edges and the surface is covered with a thin layer of ice, about 1 hour. Remove from the freezer and break up the ice with a fork, scraping it from the sides of the pan. Mix the ice shards and liquid so they are evenly distributed. Cover again and freeze for about 30 minutes. Repeat this process 3 or 4 more times until the granita is granular and icy throughout, a total time of 2–2½ hours. It should not be mushy.

Serve at once, or transfer to a freezer-safe container, cover, and freeze for up to 1 day. Granita is best served within 4 hours.

MAKES ABOUT 1½ QUARTS (48 FL OZ/1.5 L)

½ cup (4 fl oz/125 ml) water

½ cup (4 oz/125 g) sugar

1 ripe honeydew melon, about 3 lb (1.5 kg), halved and seeded

About 3 tablespoons fresh lime juice (from 1 or 2 limes)

Pinch of salt

MELONS

Nothing beats a ripe honeydew melon for pleasing sweet flavor, but finding a good one can be tricky. Honeydews are best from June to October, and as they ripen, their pale green skin turns creamy yellow. Like other muskmelons, ripe honeydews have a strong, sweet fragrance, and the ends give slightly when pressed. They do not sweeten after they have been picked. To select the best specimens, ask a greengrocer or a vendor selling them at a farmers' market to help you. Other muskmelons, such as cantaloupe, casaba, and Persian, are also delicious in this granita.

BLACKBERRY SORBET

1½ cups (12 fl oz/375 ml) water

1 cup (8 oz/250 g) sugar

3 cups (12 oz/375 g) fresh blackberries

3 tablespoons fresh lemon juice (from 1 lemon)

In a heavy saucepan, combine the water and sugar. Bring to a boil over medium-high heat and cook, stirring occasionally, until the sugar dissolves and the syrup is clear, about 1 minute.

Add the blackberries to the syrup and bring to a boil over medium-high heat. Reduce the heat to medium and simmer, stirring constantly, until the berries are soft and beginning to dissolve, about 2 minutes.

Strain the berries through a fine-mesh sieve into a bowl, pressing on the berries with the back of a large spoon. Discard the blackberry pulp and seeds.

Add the lemon juice to the blackberry syrup and stir to combine. You should have about 1½ cups (12 fl oz/375 ml) liquid. Cover and refrigerate until chilled, at least 3 hours or up to 8 hours.

Pour the blackberry syrup into an ice-cream maker and freeze according to the manufacturer's instructions. Transfer the sorbet to a freezer-safe container. Freeze until firm, at least 2 hours or up to 3 days, before serving.

Note: This sorbet does not harden as much as some of the other sorbets in this book because of the high sugar content from the berries, which inhibits hard freezing. It is meant to be enjoyed as a soft sorbet.

MAKES ABOUT 1 PINT (16 FL OZ/500 ML)

HANDLING BERRIES
Blackberries and other berry varieties are fragile and must be handled with care. Rinse them gently under cool water, discarding any that show signs of spoiling. Do not allow the berries to soak in the water for any amount of time, or they will absorb moisture and turn mushy. Spread the berries in a single layer on a double thickness of paper towels to drain. Boysenberries and loganberries are blackberry hybrids that can also be used for this sorbet. If you decide to substitute raspberries for the blackberries, handle them even more gently.

MANGO SORBET

Put the mango cubes into a bowl and mash with a fork. You should have about 2½ cups (20 fl oz/625 ml) mango pulp. Add the lemon juice and stir to combine. Cover and refrigerate until chilled, at least 2 hours or up to 8 hours.

In a small, heavy saucepan, combine the water and sugar. Bring to a boil over medium-high heat and cook, stirring occasionally, until the sugar dissolves and the syrup is clear, about 1 minute. Set aside and let cool to room temperature. Cover and refrigerate until chilled, at least 3 hours or up to 8 hours.

Add the syrup to the mango pulp and stir to combine. The mixture does not have to be smooth; it will blend during churning. Pour the mixture into an ice-cream maker and freeze according to the manufacturer's instructions. Transfer the sorbet to a freezer-safe container. Cover and freeze until firm, at least 2 hours or up to 3 days, before serving.

Note: Increase or reduce the amount of sugar by 2 tablespoons, depending on the sweetness of the mangoes.

MAKES ABOUT 1½ PINTS (24 FL OZ/750 ML)

2 perfectly ripe mangoes, about 2 lb (1 kg) total weight, cubed *(far left)*

2½ tablespoons fresh lemon juice (from 1 small lemon)

1 cup (8 fl oz/250 ml) water

¾ cup (6 oz/185 g) sugar (see Note)

CUBING MANGOES

These aromatic tropical fruits are perfectly ripe when they smell fragrant and give a little when gently pressed between your fingers. To cube, stand the mango on end. With a large, sharp knife, cut down one of the flat sides, cutting around and against the pit. You should have 1 large piece. Repeat on the other side. Place each piece flesh side up, and carefully score the flesh in a crisscross grid pattern just down to, but not piercing, the skin. Invert the slices, pressing against the center of the peel to push out the scored cubes, then cut off the cubes. Scrape the peel to remove any remaining flesh.

CRANBERRY SORBET

1½ cups (12 fl oz/375 ml) water

1½ cups (12 oz/375 g) sugar

2½ cups (20 fl oz/625 ml) unsweetened cranberry juice

In a heavy saucepan, combine the water and sugar. Bring to a boil over medium-high heat and cook, stirring occasionally, until the sugar dissolves and the syrup is clear, about 1 minute.

Pour the cranberry juice into the sugar syrup and bring to a boil over medium-high heat. Reduce the heat to medium and cook for about 1 minute. Remove from the heat and set aside to cool to room temperature.

Refrigerate the cranberry syrup until chilled, at least 3 hours or up to 8 hours.

Pour the cranberry syrup into an ice-cream maker and freeze according to the manufacturer's instructions. Transfer the sorbet to a freezer-safe container. Cover and freeze until firm, at least 2 hours or up to 3 days, before serving.

MAKES ABOUT 1 QUART (32 FL OZ/1 L)

CRANBERRIES AND THEIR JUICE

Too tart to eat raw and on their own, cranberries are delicious in sweet relishes, sauces, breads, and other preparations. Most of the autumn harvest ends up in canned cranberry sauce and bottled juice. Because cranberries marry well with other fruits, their juice often is sold mixed with apple, raspberry, or another fruit juice. It also is bottled with white grape juice to sweeten it. This sorbet calls for unsweetened juice, which can be found in natural-foods stores. The recipe adds just the right amount of sugar for a refreshing, elegant dessert.

AVOCADO ICE CREAM

In a heavy 2-qt (2-l) saucepan, combine the milk and 1 cup (8 fl oz/ 250 ml) of the cream. Cook over medium heat until bubbles form around the edges of the pan, about 5 minutes. Meanwhile, combine the egg yolks, sugar, and remaining ½ cup (4 fl oz/125 ml) cream in a bowl. Whisk until smooth.

Remove the milk mixture from the heat. Gradually whisk about ½ cup (4 fl oz/125 ml) of the hot milk mixture into the egg mixture until smooth. Pour the egg mixture into the saucepan. Cook over medium heat, stirring constantly with a wooden spoon and keeping the custard at a low simmer, until it is thick enough to coat the back of the spoon and leaves a clear trail when a finger is drawn through it, 4–6 minutes. Do not let the custard boil. Strain through a fine-mesh sieve into a bowl.

Place the bowl in a larger bowl partially filled with ice cubes and water. Stir occasionally until cool. Cover with plastic wrap, pressing it directly on the surface of the custard to prevent a skin from forming. Refrigerate until chilled, at least 3 hours or up to 24 hours.

Pit the avocados *(left)* and scrape the avocado flesh into a food processor. Add the custard and pulse 4 or 5 times to mix. Add the lime juice and pulse 1 or 2 times to blend. Scrape the avocado mixture into a nonaluminum bowl. Cover with plastic wrap, pressing it directly on the surface. Refrigerate until chilled, at least 30 minutes or up to 2 hours.

Pour the avocado mixture into an ice-cream maker and freeze according to the manufacturer's instructions. Transfer the ice cream to a freezer-safe container. Cover and freeze until firm, at least 3 hours or up to 2 days, before serving.

MAKES ABOUT 1 QUART (32 FL OZ/1 L)

1½ cups (12 fl oz/375 ml) whole milk

1½ cups (12 fl oz/375 ml) heavy (double) cream

5 large egg yolks

¾ cup (6 oz/185 g) sugar

2 very ripe Hass avocados, about 1 lb (500 g) total weight

2 teaspoons fresh lime juice

PITTING AVOCADOS

To pit an avocado, use a small, sharp knife to cut it in half lengthwise, cutting around the large center pit. Rotate the halves in opposite directions to separate them. Scoop out the pit with the tip of a spoon. Alternatively, set the avocado half with the pit on a work surface, carefully strike the pit with the wide end of a sharp knife so that the blade lodges in it, and then twist the knife and draw out the pit. To remove the flesh, ease a large spoon between the flesh and the peel. Once most of the flesh has been removed, turn the skin inside out to scrape as closely to the peel as possible.

COFFEE, TEA, AND NUTS

In this chapter, the sophisticated flavors of espresso and green tea are matched by the complex taste and texture of hazelnuts, pistachios, and pecans. When these ingredients are churned into rich, creamy homemade desserts, the results are extraordinary. Make these frozen desserts when you are looking for something slightly unusual and subtly extravagant.

COFFEE GRANITA

SWEETENED
WHIPPED CREAM

When whipping cream, begin
by chilling your equipment,
including a metal bowl and the
beaters, and use well-chilled
cream to yield the best results.

Using an electric mixer on
medium-high speed, beat 1 cup
(8 fl oz/250 ml) heavy (double)
cream until thick. Continue
beating while adding 1 tablespoon confectioners' (icing)
sugar until the cream forms
soft, luxuriant peaks when the
beaters are turned upright,
2–3 minutes. Use the whipped
cream immediately. Makes
about 2 cups (16 fl oz/500 ml).

In a small, heavy saucepan, combine 2 cups (16 fl oz/500 ml) of the water and the granulated sugar. Bring to a boil over medium-high heat and cook, stirring occasionally, until the sugar dissolves and the syrup is clear, about 1 minute. Set aside to cool slightly.

In another saucepan, combine the remaining 2 cups (16 fl oz/ 500 ml) water and the ground coffee. Bring to a boil over medium-high heat. Remove from the heat and add the lemon zest. Let steep for about 5 minutes.

Strain the coffee mixture through a coffee filter into a bowl. Add the sugar syrup and lemon juice and stir to mix. Cover the mixture and refrigerate until chilled, at least 3 hours or up to 8 hours.

Pour the mixture into a shallow pan that will fit in the freezer. The best size is a 9-by-13-inch (23-by-33-cm) jelly-roll pan. Cover with aluminum foil and freeze until the mixture begins to harden around the edges and the surface is covered with a thin layer of ice, about 1 hour. Remove the pan from the freezer and break up the ice with a fork, scraping it from the sides of the pan. Mix the ice shards and liquid so they are evenly distributed. Cover again and freeze for about 30 minutes.

Repeat this process 3 or 4 more times until the granita is granular and icy throughout, a total time of 2–2½ hours. It should not be mushy.

Serve at once in tall glasses layered with Sweetened Whipped Cream, ending with a soft swirl of cream. Garnish with chocolate-covered coffee beans or a dusting of cocoa powder, if desired. If not serving at once, transfer the granita to a freezer-safe container, cover, and freeze for up to 24 hours. Granita is best served on the day it's made, preferably within 4 hours of freezing.

MAKES ABOUT 1 QUART (32 FL OZ/1 L)

4 cups (32 fl oz/1 l) water

2 cups (1 lb/500 g) granulated sugar

½ cup (1½ oz/45 g) finely ground dark-roast coffee beans (page 14)

Zest of 1 lemon, coarsely chopped

3 tablespoons fresh lemon juice (from 1 lemon)

Sweetened Whipped Cream (far left) for serving

Chocolate-covered coffee beans or cocoa powder for garnish (optional)

HONEY-PECAN ICE CREAM

½ cup (2 oz/60 g) pecans, plus extra for optional garnish

½ cup (6 oz/180 g) honey

1½ cups (12 fl oz/375 ml) whole milk

1½ cups (12 fl oz/375 ml) heavy (double) cream

4 large egg yolks

¼ cup (2 oz/60 g) sugar

1 teaspoon vanilla extract (essence)

In a dry frying pan, toast the ½ cup pecans over medium-high heat, shaking the pan, until lightly browned and fragrant, 2–3 minutes. Transfer to a plate to cool, then chop coarsely.

In a small, heavy saucepan, heat ¼ cup (3 oz/90 g) of the honey over medium heat for 3–4 minutes, whisking constantly. Gradually whisk in the milk and 1 cup (8 fl oz/250 ml) of the cream, again whisking constantly. The honey may ball up when the milk is added; keep whisking until smooth. Cook, whisking occasionally, until bubbles form around the edges of the pan, 3–4 minutes.

Meanwhile, combine the egg yolks, sugar, and remaining ½ cup (4 fl oz/125 ml) cream in a bowl. Whisk until smooth. Gradually whisk about ½ cup (4 fl oz/ 125 ml) of the hot milk mixture into the egg mixture until smooth. Pour the egg mixture into the saucepan. Cook over medium heat, stirring constantly with a wooden spoon and keeping the custard at a low simmer, until it is thick enough to coat the back of the spoon and leaves a clear trail when a finger is drawn through it, 4–6 minutes. Do not let the custard boil. Strain through a fine-mesh sieve into a bowl. Stir in the vanilla.

Place the bowl in a larger bowl partially filled with ice cubes and water. Stir occasionally until cool. Cover with plastic wrap, pressing it directly on the surface of the custard to prevent a skin from forming. Refrigerate until chilled, at least 3 hours or up to 24 hours.

Pour the custard into an ice-cream maker and freeze according to the manufacturer's instructions. When nearly frozen and the consistency of thick whipped cream, add the remaining ¼ cup (3 oz/90 g) honey and the pecans. Churn or stir until just mixed. Transfer the ice cream to a freezer-safe container. Cover and freeze until firm, at least 3 hours or up to 3 days, before serving. If desired, garnish each serving with whole and/or chopped pecans.

MAKES ABOUT 1 QUART (32 FL OZ/1 L)

HONEY VARIETIES

Clover honey is the variety most people are familiar with, but it is not the only type of honey available. Depending on the source of the nectar, honey ranges from almost white to deep, rich brown. In general, the lighter the color, the more delicate the flavor. The flavor also varies according to the plants that surround the hive. Possible varieties include light, mild alfalfa, lavender, raspberry, or orange blossom, as well as stronger buckwheat, eucalyptus, or tupelo. For this ice cream, use a light clover or orange blossom honey.

CHOCOLATE-HAZELNUT GELATO

TOASTING AND SKINNING HAZELNUTS

Position a rack in the center of the oven and preheat the oven to 350°F (180°C). In a shallow roasting pan, spread the hazelnuts in a single layer and toast, shaking the pan 2 or 3 times during toasting, until the nuts are golden beneath their skins, 10–15 minutes. To check for doneness, remove a hazelnut from the oven after about 10 minutes and cut it open. Check every few minutes until the nuts are golden brown all the way through. Wrap the hot hazelnuts in a clean kitchen towel and let cool completely. Rub the nuts in the towel to remove the loose skins.

To make the hazelnut paste, combine the ¾ cup hazelnuts, hazelnut oil, sugar, and salt in a food processor. Process until a thick paste forms, about 2 minutes. Transfer to a bowl and set aside. You should have about ⅓ cup (3 oz/90 g) paste (see Note).

In a heavy 2-qt (2-l) saucepan, combine the milk and hazelnut paste. Cook over medium heat until bubbles form around the edges of the pan, about 5 minutes. Do not let the mixture boil.

Meanwhile, combine the egg yolks, cream, sugar, and salt in a bowl. Whisk until smooth and the sugar begins to dissolve. Remove the milk mixture from the heat. Gradually whisk about ½ cup (4 fl oz/ 125 ml) of the hot milk mixture into the egg mixture until smooth. Pour the egg mixture into the saucepan. Cook over medium heat, stirring constantly with a wooden spoon and keeping the custard at a low simmer, until it is thick enough to coat the back of the spoon and leaves a clear trail when a finger is drawn through it, 4–6 minutes. Do not let the custard boil.

Put the chopped chocolate in a heatproof bowl and pour the hot custard over it. Stir until smooth. Strain through a fine-mesh sieve into a bowl. Place the bowl in a larger bowl partially filled with ice cubes and water. Stir occasionally until cool. Cover with plastic wrap, pressing it directly on the surface of the custard. Refrigerate until chilled, at least 3 hours or up to 24 hours.

Pour the custard into an ice-cream maker and freeze according to the manufacturer's instructions. Transfer the gelato to a freezer-safe container. Cover and freeze until firm, at least 4 hours or up to 3 days, before serving. If desired, garnish each serving with chopped hazelnuts.

Note: You may use ⅓ cup (3 oz/90 g) commercial hazelnut paste in place of the homemade paste in this recipe.

MAKES ABOUT 1 QUART (32 FL OZ/1 L)

FOR THE HAZELNUT PASTE:

¾ cup (3½ oz/105 g) hazelnuts (filberts), toasted and skinned *(far left)*, plus extra, coarsely chopped, for optional garnish

1 tablespoon hazelnut oil or canola oil

1 tablespoon sugar

Pinch of salt

3 cups (24 fl oz/750 ml) whole milk

4 large egg yolks

½ cup (4 fl oz/125 ml) heavy (double) cream

¾ cup (6 oz/185 g) sugar

Pinch of salt

4½ oz (140 g) bittersweet or semisweet (plain) chocolate, coarsely chopped

PISTACHIO AND DRIED CHERRY ICE CREAM

1½ cups (12 fl oz/375 ml) whole milk

1½ cups (12 fl oz/375 ml) heavy (double) cream

1 cup (4 oz/125 g) coarsely chopped unsalted pistachios

1 cup (4 oz/125 g) coarsely chopped dried cherries

4 large egg yolks

½ cup (4 oz/125 g) sugar

½ teaspoon vanilla extract (essence)

In a heavy 2-qt (2-l) saucepan, combine the milk, 1 cup (8 fl oz/250 ml) of the cream, ½ cup (2 oz/60 g) of the pistachios, and ½ cup (2 oz/60 g) of the cherries. Cook over medium heat until bubbles form around the edges of the pan, about 5 minutes. Remove from the heat and set aside for 20 minutes to steep.

Strain the milk mixture through a fine-mesh sieve into a bowl, pressing on the solids with the back of a large spoon. Discard the pistachios and cherries. Return the milk to the saucepan.

Meanwhile, combine the egg yolks, sugar, and remaining ½ cup (4 fl oz/125 ml) cream in a bowl. Whisk until smooth.

Gradually whisk about ½ cup (4 fl oz/125 ml) of the warm milk mixture into the egg mixture until smooth. Pour the egg mixture into the saucepan. Cook over medium heat, stirring constantly with a wooden spoon and keeping the custard at a low simmer, until it is thick enough to coat the back of the spoon and leaves a clear trail when a finger is drawn through it, 4–6 minutes. Do not let the custard boil. Strain through a fine-mesh sieve into a bowl. Add the vanilla and stir to combine.

Place the bowl in a larger bowl partially filled with ice cubes and water. Stir occasionally until cool. Cover with plastic wrap, pressing it directly on the surface to prevent a skin from forming. Refrigerate until chilled, at least 3 hours or up to 24 hours. In a small bowl, toss the remaining pistachios and cherries together.

Pour the custard into an ice-cream maker and freeze according to the manufacturer's instructions. When nearly frozen and the consistency of thick whipped cream, add the remaining pistachios and cherries. Churn or stir just until mixed. Transfer the ice cream to a freezer-safe container. Cover and freeze until firm, at least 3 hours or up to 3 days, before serving.

MAKES ABOUT 1 QUART (32 FL OZ/1 L)

PISTACHIOS

Pistachios, used widely throughout the Middle East and India, are also appreciated in other parts of the world. When the nuts are used to flavor ice cream, they imbue it with an indescribable richness. For this recipe, purchase nuts that have not been salted or dyed red. Because the shells crack open as the nuts ripen, pistachios are easy to shell. Rub off the interior skins with your fingers or a kitchen towel. Pistachios are also available already shelled.

GREEN TEA ICE CREAM

GREEN TEA

Green tea is made from steamed and dried tea leaves that, unlike the leaves for black tea, have not been fermented. Its delicate flavor translates to a light, refreshing ice cream. After a day or two, the acids that occur naturally in the tea become more pronounced, so it is best to eat the ice cream soon after making it. Though convenient, tea bags do not make the best tea, as the leaves are not able to circulate. For better flavor, seek out high-quality loose tea sold at tea shops or specialty-food stores. Avoid common commercial brands, which are made from blends of inferior bits of leaves.

In a heavy 2-qt (2-l) saucepan, cook the milk over medium heat until bubbles form around the edges of the pan, about 5 minutes. Remove from the heat and stir in the loose tea or submerge the tea bags in the hot milk. Let cool to room temperature, then cover and refrigerate for at least 4 hours or up to overnight.

Strain the milk through a fine-mesh sieve into a bowl or remove the tea bags from the milk, gently squeezing them to extract their liquid. In a heavy 2-qt (2-l) saucepan, combine the tea-infused milk and 1 cup (8 fl oz/250 ml) of the cream. Cook over medium heat until bubbles form around the edges of the pan, about 5 minutes.

Meanwhile, combine the egg yolks, sugar, and remaining ½ cup (4 fl oz/125 ml) cream in a bowl. Whisk until the sugar dissolves. Gradually whisk about ½ cup (4 fl oz/125 ml) of the hot milk mixture into the egg mixture until smooth. Pour the egg mixture into the saucepan and add the honey. Cook over medium heat, stirring constantly with a wooden spoon and keeping the custard at a low simmer, until it is thick enough to coat the back of the spoon and leaves a clear trail when a finger is drawn through it, 4–6 minutes. Do not let boil. Strain through a fine-mesh sieve into a bowl.

Place the bowl in a larger bowl partially filled with ice cubes and water. Stir occasionally until cool. Cover with plastic wrap, pressing it directly on the surface of the custard to prevent a skin from forming. Refrigerate until chilled, at least 3 hours or up to 24 hours.

Pour the custard into an ice-cream maker and freeze according to the manufacturer's instructions. Transfer the ice cream to a freezer-safe container. Cover and freeze until firm, at least 3 hours or up to 2 days, before serving.

Note: If using loose tea, you will need to use 2 cups milk; if using tea bags, use 1½ cups milk.

MAKES ABOUT 1 QUART (32 FL OZ/1 L)

1½–2 cups (12–16 fl oz/ 375–500 ml) whole milk (see Note)

2 tablespoons loose green tea or 6 green tea bags

1½ cups (12 fl oz/375 ml) heavy (double) cream

5 large egg yolks

¾ cup (6 oz/185 g) sugar

3 tablespoons honey

ESPRESSO ICE CREAM
WITH DARK CHOCOLATE CHUNKS

1½ cups (12 fl oz / 375 ml) whole milk

1½ cups (12 fl oz / 375 ml) heavy (double) cream

1 cup (8 fl oz / 250 ml) brewed espresso

4 large egg yolks

½ cup (4 oz / 125 g) sugar

5 oz (155 g) bittersweet or semisweet (plain) chocolate, chopped into ½-inch (12-mm) chunks

In a heavy 2-qt (2-l) saucepan, combine the milk, 1 cup (8 fl oz/ 250 ml) of the cream, and the espresso. Bring to a low simmer over medium heat and cook until slightly thickened, about 20 minutes. Do not let boil. If it does, remove from the heat, stir to cool it down, then return to low heat.

Meanwhile, combine the egg yolks, sugar, and remaining ½ cup (4 fl oz / 125 ml) cream in a bowl. Whisk until smooth.

Remove the milk mixture from the heat. Gradually whisk about ½ cup (4 fl oz / 125 ml) of the milk mixture into the egg mixture until smooth. Pour the egg mixture into the saucepan. Cook over medium heat, stirring constantly with a wooden spoon and keeping the custard at a low simmer, until it is thick enough to coat the back of the spoon and leaves a clear trail when a finger is drawn through it, 4–6 minutes. Do not let the custard boil. Strain through a fine-mesh sieve into a bowl.

Place the bowl in a larger bowl partially filled with ice cubes and water. Stir occasionally until cool. Cover with plastic wrap, pressing it directly on the surface of the custard to prevent a skin from forming. Refrigerate until chilled, at least 3 hours or up to 24 hours.

Pour the custard into an ice-cream maker and freeze according to the manufacturer's instructions. When nearly frozen and the consistency of thick whipped cream, add the chocolate chunks. Churn or stir just until mixed. Transfer the ice cream to a freezer-safe container. Cover and freeze until firm, at least 3 hours or up to 3 days, before serving.

Serving Tip: To embellish this ice cream, serve it with Fudge Sauce (page 82) or Caramel Sauce (page 113).

MAKES ABOUT 1 QUART (32 FL OZ / 1 L)

BREWING ESPRESSO

Espresso, which is brewed with dark-roasted beans, is appreciated for its robust, rich, intense coffee flavor. Most espresso aficionados sip their beloved beverage black and bitter from small cups, but when it is paired with cream and chocolate, espresso becomes a tempting ice cream. If you make the ice cream with coffee brewed from freshly ground beans instead of instant espresso powder or granules, the flavor will be as deep and as satisfying as a cup of espresso after a fine meal.

TOASTED COCONUT ICE CREAM

In a heavy 2-qt (2-l) saucepan, combine the milk, 1 cup (8 fl oz/ 250 ml) of the cream, and ¾ cup (3 oz/90 g) of the coconut. Cook over medium heat until bubbles form around the edges of the pan, about 5 minutes. Set aside for 20 minutes, then strain through a fine-mesh sieve into a bowl, pressing against the coconut. Return the milk mixture to the pan and place over medium heat until bubbles form around the edges of the pan, about 5 minutes.

Meanwhile, combine the egg yolks, sugar, and remaining ½ cup (4 fl oz/125 ml) cream in a bowl. Whisk until smooth. Gradually whisk about ½ cup (4 fl oz/125 ml) of the hot milk mixture into the egg mixture until smooth. Pour the egg mixture into the saucepan. Cook over medium heat, stirring constantly with a wooden spoon at a low simmer, until the custard is thick enough to coat the back of the spoon and leaves a clear trail when a finger is drawn through it, 4–6 minutes. Do not let the custard boil. Remove from the heat. Stir in the cream of coconut. Strain through a fine-mesh sieve into a bowl. Stir in the vanilla.

Place the bowl in a larger bowl partially filled with ice cubes and water. Stir occasionally until cool. Cover with plastic wrap, pressing it directly on the surface. Refrigerate for at least 3 hours or up to 24 hours. Meanwhile, toast the remaining ½ cup (2 oz/60 g) coconut, plus up to ¼ cup (1 oz/30 g) extra for garnish (if using), in a small, dry frying pan over medium-high heat, stirring occasionally, until lightly browned, 1–2 minutes. Transfer to a plate to cool.

Pour the custard into an ice-cream maker and freeze according to the manufacturer's instructions. When it is the consistency of thick whipped cream, add the ½ cup toasted coconut. Churn or stir until just mixed. Transfer to a freezer-safe container. Cover and freeze until firm, at least 3 hours or up to 3 days, before serving. If desired, garnish each serving with toasted coconut.

MAKES ABOUT 1 QUART (32 FL OZ/1 L)

COCONUT

This recipe uses sweetened shredded coconut, sold in plastic bags in the baking aisle of most supermarkets. Costlier canned coconut is moister, but its use here would make little difference since the coconut is steeped in liquid as a first step in this recipe. When you look for canned cream of coconut, be sure to pick the right product. Don't buy coconut milk; instead, purchase the thick, sweetened product used in tropical drinks like piña coladas. If you like coconut and chocolate, add chocolate chips with the toasted coconut, or serve the ice cream with Hardening Hot Fudge Sauce (page 112).

1½ cups (12 fl oz/375 ml) whole milk

1½ cups (12 fl oz/375 ml) heavy (double) cream

1¼ cups (5 oz/150 g) sweetened shredded coconut, plus extra for optional garnish

4 large egg yolks

1 cup (8 oz/250 g) sugar

3 tablespoons cream of coconut

1 teaspoon vanilla extract (essence)

ELEGANT ICE CREAMS

If you are looking for a stylish finish for your next dinner party, or you want to serve a light palate cleanser between courses, look no further than the list below. Ice cream vibrant with berries or enlivened with ginger or mint will end any dinner with a flourish, while a refreshing fruit granita or sorbet will pleasantly introduce, politely interrupt, or gracefully conclude a meal.

BLUEBERRIES AND CREAM
58

AMARETTO ICE CREAM
61

GINGER ICE CREAM
62

RASPBERRY ICE CREAM
65

PEPPERMINT ICE CREAM
66

TANGERINE SORBET
69

PINK GRAPEFRUIT GRANITA
WITH CHAMPAGNE
70

BLUEBERRIES AND CREAM

In a heavy 2-qt (2-l) saucepan, combine the fresh blueberries, water, and sugar. Bring to a boil over medium-high heat, stirring occasionally to help dissolve the sugar. Reduce the heat to medium and simmer for about 1 minute. Remove from the heat and let stand for 30 minutes to steep.

Transfer the blueberry mixture to a food processor. Process until smooth, about 1 minute. Strain through a fine-mesh sieve into a bowl. Cover and refrigerate until chilled, at least 3 hours or up to 24 hours.

Add the cream and lemon juice to the blueberry purée and stir to combine.

Pour the mixture into an ice-cream maker and freeze according to the manufacturer's instructions. Transfer to a freezer-safe container. Cover and freeze until firm, at least 3 hours or up to 3 days, before serving.

Note: If using frozen blueberries, make the sugar syrup by combining the water and sugar in a saucepan, bringing the mixture to a boil over medium-high heat, and cooking it until clear, about 1 minute. Put the frozen blueberries in a heatproof bowl and pour the syrup over them. Let cool and then transfer to the food processor. Proceed with the recipe.

MAKES ABOUT 1 QUART (32 FL OZ/1 L)

2 cups (8 oz/250 g) fresh blueberries or frozen blueberries (see Note)

¾ cup (6 fl oz/180 ml) water

1 cup (8 oz/250 g) sugar

1 cup (8 fl oz/250 ml) heavy (double) cream

1 tablespoon fresh lemon juice

BLUEBERRIES

Most blueberries are large and round with deep blue skins and a powdery white bloom. In season from late spring until the end of the summer, they are a delicious treat when warm weather arrives. Like all berries, blueberries freeze beautifully, so if you cannot find fresh ones, use frozen. Tiny, sweet Maine blueberries are especially good. These low-bush berries, famous for growing wild in Maine and similar cool climates, do not travel well, although nowadays a fairly good-sized crop is cultivated and sold frozen or made into preserves.

AMARETTO ICE CREAM

1½ cups (12 fl oz/375 ml) whole milk

1½ cups (12 fl oz/375 ml) heavy (double) cream

⅓ cup (3 fl oz/80 ml) amaretto liqueur

4 large egg yolks

½ cup (4 oz/125 g) sugar

Pinch of salt

½ cup (1½ oz/45 g) crumbled amaretti cookies, about 30 cookies

In a heavy 2-qt (2-l) saucepan, combine the milk, 1 cup (8 fl oz/ 250 ml) of the cream, and the amaretto. Cook over medium heat until bubbles form around the edges of the pan, about 5 minutes.

Meanwhile, combine the egg yolks, sugar, salt, and remaining ½ cup (4 fl oz/125 ml) cream in a bowl. Whisk until the mixture is smooth and the sugar begins to dissolve.

Remove the milk mixture from the heat. Gradually whisk about ½ cup (4 fl oz/125 ml) of the hot milk mixture into the egg mixture, whisking constantly, until smooth. Pour the egg mixture into the saucepan. Cook over medium heat, stirring constantly with a wooden spoon and keeping the custard at a low simmer, until it is thick enough to coat the back of the spoon and leaves a clear trail when a finger is drawn through it, 4–6 minutes. Do not let the custard boil. Strain through a fine-mesh sieve into a bowl.

Place the bowl in a larger bowl partially filled with ice cubes and water. Stir occasionally until cool. Cover with plastic wrap, pressing it directly on the surface of the custard to prevent a skin from forming. Refrigerate until chilled, at least 3 hours or up to 24 hours.

Pour the custard into an ice-cream maker and freeze according to the manufacturer's instructions. When nearly frozen and the consistency of thick whipped cream, add the crumbled amaretti. Churn or stir just until mixed. Transfer the ice cream to a freezer-safe container. Cover and freeze until firm, at least 3 hours or up to 3 days before serving.

MAKES ABOUT 1 QUART (32 FL OZ/1 L)

AMARETTO AND AMARETTI

Amaretto, a liqueur that tastes of almonds, and amaretti, almond-flavored cookies, both originated in Italy, where this flavor component is greatly prized for use in baked goods and desserts. Both products are attributed to the Italian town of Saronno, which explains why Amaretto di Saronno and Amaretti di Saronno are considered to be the most authentic. Today, the liqueur and the cookies are also made in other parts of the world, and very often are flavored with apricot kernels instead of bitter almonds, since the taste is similar.

GINGER ICE CREAM

In a heavy 2-qt (2-l) saucepan, combine the milk, 1 cup (8 fl oz/250 ml) of the cream, and the fresh ginger. Cook over medium heat until bubbles form around the edges of the pan, about 5 minutes. Remove from the heat and let stand for 20 minutes to steep.

Meanwhile, combine the egg yolks, sugar, salt, and remaining ½ cup (4 fl oz/125 ml) cream in a bowl. Whisk until the mixture is smooth and the sugar begins to dissolve.

Gradually whisk about ½ cup (4 fl oz/125 ml) of the warm milk mixture into the egg mixture, whisking constantly, until smooth. Pour the egg mixture into the saucepan. Cook over medium heat, stirring constantly with a wooden spoon and keeping the custard at a low simmer, until it is thick enough to coat the back of the spoon and leaves a clear trail when a finger is drawn through it, 4–6 minutes. Do not let the custard boil. Strain through a fine-mesh sieve into a bowl.

Place the bowl in a larger bowl partially filled with ice cubes and water. Stir occasionally until cool. Cover with plastic wrap, pressing it directly on the surface of the custard to prevent a skin from forming. Refrigerate until chilled, at least 3 hours or up to 24 hours.

Pour the custard into an ice-cream maker and freeze according to the manufacturer's instructions. When nearly frozen and the consistency of thick whipped cream, add the 2½ tablespoons candied ginger. Churn or stir just until mixed. Transfer the ice cream to a freezer-safe container. Cover and freeze until firm, at least 3 hours or up to 3 days, before serving. Garnish with candied ginger and/or with gingersnaps, if desired.

MAKES ABOUT 1 QUART (32 FL OZ/1 L)

GINGER

The slightly sharp, slightly sweet flavor of ginger generates a spicy warmth that deliciously complements the coolness of ice cream. Slices of fresh ginger infuse the milk and cream with subtle flavor that is further enhanced by crunchy, chopped candied ginger added later to the ice cream. Look for firm, thin-skinned, beige-colored fresh ginger in supermarkets. Candied ginger, also called crystallized ginger, is sold in supermarkets and health-food stores.

1½ cups (12 fl oz/375 ml) whole milk

1½ cups (12 fl oz/375 ml) heavy (double) cream

1 piece (2 inches/5 cm) fresh ginger, peeled, cut into slices ¼ inch (6 mm) thick, and coarsely chopped (about ⅓ cup/2 oz/60 g)

6 large egg yolks

½ cup (4 oz/125 g) plus 2 tablespoons sugar

Pinch of salt

2½ tablespoons minced candied (crystallized) ginger, plus extra chopped candied ginger for garnish

Gingersnaps for garnish (optional)

RASPBERRY ICE CREAM

1 cup (8 fl oz/250 ml)
whole milk

1 cup (8 fl oz/250 ml)
heavy (double) cream

3 large egg yolks

¾ cup (6 oz/185 g) sugar

2 cups (8 oz/250 g) fresh
or partially thawed frozen
raspberries

Crystallized flowers or
fruits for garnish *(far right)*

In a heavy 2-qt (2-l) saucepan, combine the milk and ½ cup (4 fl oz/250 ml) of the cream. Cook over medium heat until bubbles form around the edges of the pan, about 5 minutes.

Meanwhile, combine the egg yolks, ½ cup (4 oz/125 g) of the sugar, and remaining ½ cup (4 fl oz/125 ml) cream in a bowl. Whisk until the mixture is smooth and the sugar begins to dissolve.

Remove the milk mixture from the heat. Gradually whisk about ½ cup (4 fl oz/125 ml) of the hot milk mixture into the egg mixture until smooth. Pour the egg mixture into the saucepan. Cook over medium heat, stirring constantly with a wooden spoon and keeping the custard at a low simmer, until it is thick enough to coat the back of the spoon and leaves a clear trail when a finger is drawn through it, 4–6 minutes. Do not let the custard boil. Strain through a fine-mesh sieve into a bowl.

Place the bowl in a larger bowl partially filled with ice cubes and water. Stir occasionally until the custard is cool.

Put the raspberries and the remaining ¼ cup (2 oz/60 g) sugar in a food processor fitted with a metal blade and process until smooth. Strain the berries through a fine-mesh sieve into a clean bowl, gently pushing on the berries with the back of a spoon. Discard the raspberry pulp and seeds. Add the raspberry juice to the custard and stir to combine. Cover with plastic wrap, pressing it directly on the surface to prevent a skin from forming. Refrigerate until chilled, at least 3 hours or up to 24 hours.

Pour the custard into an ice-cream maker and freeze according to the manufacturer's instructions. Transfer the ice cream to a freezer-safe container. Cover and freeze until firm, at least 3 hours or up to 3 days, before serving. Garnish each serving with crystallized flowers or fruits.

MAKES ABOUT 1 QUART (32 FL OZ/1 L)

CRYSTALLIZED GARNISHES

Crystallized edible flowers, such as pansies and rose petals, or small fruits, such as grapes and berries, make lovely garnishes for ice cream. To make enough garnishes for 6 to 8 servings, lightly beat a large egg white and have 1½ cups (10½ oz/ 330 g) superfine (caster) sugar on hand. Dip the flowers or fruit in the egg white or brush it on with a small pastry brush. Let the excess run off and generously dust with the sugar. Set on racks to dry for at least 6 hours or overnight. Note that these garnishes contain uncooked egg whites. For more information, see page 114.

PEPPERMINT ICE CREAM

In a bowl, stir the cream and sugar together until the sugar dissolves. Add the vanilla and stir to combine. Set aside for about 15 minutes, stirring occasionally, to allow the flavors to blend. Cover and refrigerate until chilled, at least 3 hours or up to 8 hours.

In a food processor, grind the peppermint candies by pulsing 2 or 3 times. Some of the candies will be more finely ground than others; small chunks of candy will add texture and interest to the final ice cream.

Pour the cream mixture into an ice-cream maker and freeze according to the manufacturer's instructions. When nearly frozen and the consistency of thick whipped cream, add the ground peppermint candies. Churn or stir just until mixed. Transfer the ice cream to a freezer-safe container. Cover and freeze until firm, at least 3 hours or up to 3 days, before serving.

Note: This ice cream does not harden as much as some of the other recipes in this book because of the high sugar content from the candies, which inhibits hard freezing. It is meant to be enjoyed as a soft ice cream.

MAKES ABOUT 1 QUART (32 FL OZ/1 L)

3 cups (24 fl oz/750 ml) heavy (double) cream

1¼ cups (10 oz/315 g) sugar

2½ teaspoons vanilla extract (essence)

About 36 hard peppermint candies (6 oz/185 g)

PEPPERMINT

Along with spearmint, peppermint is one of the most common and popular varieties of mint, of which there are more than thirty different types. Stronger than spearmint, peppermint has a spicy and tangy flavor. Candies flavored with peppermint have become traditional favorites, whether in the form of candy canes during the holidays or as red-and-white hard candies, often called starlights, at other times during the year. The candies derive their flavor from peppermint oil, a highly concentrated oil that is also used to treat indigestion.

TANGERINE SORBET

1 cup (8 fl oz/250 ml) water

½ cup (4 oz/125 g) sugar (see Note)

1 tablespoon grated tangerine zest

2 cups (16 fl oz/500 ml) fresh tangerine juice (from 5 or 6 large tangerines)

In a small, heavy saucepan, combine the water and sugar. Bring to a boil over medium-high heat and cook, stirring occasionally, until the sugar dissolves and the syrup is clear, about 1 minute.

Remove the syrup from the heat and add the tangerine zest. Let stand for 20 minutes to steep. Cover and refrigerate until chilled, 2–3 hours.

Strain the tangerine juice through a fine-mesh sieve into a non-aluminum bowl. Cover and refrigerate until chilled, 2–3 hours.

Stir the tangerine juice and syrup together. Pour into an ice cream maker and freeze according to the manufacturer's instructions. When frozen, transfer the sorbet to a freezer-safe container. Cover and freeze the sorbet until firm, at least 3 hours or up to 3 days, before serving.

Note: Increase or decrease the amount of sugar by 2–3 tablespoons depending on the sweetness of the tangerines. This sorbet is meant to be pleasantly tangy.

MAKES ABOUT 1 QUART (32 FL OZ/1 L)

TANGERINES

Tangerines are flavorful citrus fruits that are generally divided into sections and eaten out of hand. Wonderfully juicy and sweet, they make exceptional sorbet. The names *tangerine* and *mandarin orange* are interchangeable, and among the most common varieties of the fruit is the Florida-grown, red-orange Dancy. Another familiar member of the family is the small Clementine. A tangelo is a cross between a mandarin and a pomelo, an ancestor of the grapefruit, with the Minneola a popular variety. Tangelos or oranges could also be used in this recipe. They will yield a more mild sorbet.

PINK GRAPEFRUIT GRANITA
WITH CHAMPAGNE

In a small, heavy saucepan, combine the water and sugar. Bring to a boil over medium-high heat and cook, stirring occasionally, until the sugar dissolves and the syrup is clear, about 1 minute. Remove from the heat and let cool to room temperature, about 30 minutes.

Stir the grapefruit juice into the syrup. Cover and refrigerate until chilled, 2–3 hours.

Stir the Champagne into the syrup. Add the grenadine, if using.

Pour the mixture into a shallow pan that will fit in the freezer. The best size is a 9-by-13-inch (23-by-33-cm) jelly-roll pan. Cover with aluminum foil and freeze until the mixture begins to harden around the edges and the surface is covered with a thin layer of ice, about 1 hour. Remove the pan from the freezer and break up the ice with a fork, scraping it from the sides of the pan. Mix the ice shards and liquid so they are evenly distributed. Cover again and freeze for about 30 minutes.

Repeat this process 3 or 4 more times until the granita is granular and icy throughout, a total time of 2–2½ hours. It should not be mushy.

Serve at once, or transfer the granita to a freezer-safe container, cover, and freeze for up to 24 hours. Granita is best served the day it is made, preferably within 4 hours of freezing.

Note: Grenadine is a sweet, red pomegranate-flavored syrup. It will boost the color of this granita.

MAKES ABOUT 1½ QUARTS (48 FL OZ/1.5 L)

1 cup (8 fl oz/250 ml) water

1 cup (8 oz/250 g) sugar

1½ cups (12 fl oz/375 ml) pink grapefruit juice (from 2 grapefruits)

½ cup (4 fl oz/125 ml) Champagne, chilled

1–2 teaspoons grenadine (optional; see Note)

CHAMPAGNE

While genuine Champagne is made in the region of France of the same name, many other countries produce excellent sparkling wines that are as bubbly and appealing. Look for Prosecco from Italy, Cava from Spain, Sekt from Germany, and sparkling wines from the United States and Australia. Whatever your choice, store the wine in a cool spot and chill it for a few hours before using. No sparkling wine retains its effervescence for long, so be prepared to serve what you do not use in the recipe.

INDULGENT ICE CREAMS

When nothing but a bona fide treat will do, try one of these ice creams. Blend tangy crème fraîche with candied citrus zest for a rich dessert, transform zabaglione into a Marsala-scented gelato, or combine pumpkin and warm spice for a special holiday treat. Of course, chocolate ice cream, whether layered with fudge or paired with raspberry, is the very definition of indulgent.

ROCKY ROAD ICE CREAM
74

WHITE CHOCOLATE ICE CREAM
77

CARAMEL ICE CREAM
78

PUMPKIN ICE CREAM
81

CHOCOLATE FUDGE SWIRL ICE CREAM
82

CRÈME FRAÎCHE ICE CREAM
WITH CANDIED LEMON ZEST
85

ZABAGLIONE GELATO
86

CHOCOLATE-RASPBERRY TRUFFLE ICE CREAM
88

ROCKY ROAD ICE CREAM

In a heavy 2-qt (2-l) saucepan, combine the milk and 1 cup (8 fl oz/250 ml) of the cream. Cook over medium heat until bubbles form around the edges of the pan, about 5 minutes.

Put the coarsely chopped chocolate in a heatproof bowl. Pour the hot milk mixture over the chocolate and let stand until melted, about 3 minutes. (Set the saucepan aside for later use.) Whisk until the mixture is smooth.

Meanwhile, in a separate bowl, combine the egg yolks, sugar, salt, and remaining ½ cup (4 fl oz/125 ml) cream. Whisk until the mixture is smooth and the sugar begins to dissolve.

Gradually whisk about ½ cup (4 fl oz/125 ml) of the warm milk mixture into the egg mixture until smooth. Pour the egg mixture into the reserved saucepan and stir in the remaining milk mixture. Cook over medium heat, stirring constantly with a wooden spoon and keeping the custard at a low simmer, until it is thick enough to coat the back of the spoon and leaves a clear trail when a finger is drawn through it, 4–6 minutes. Do not let the custard boil. Strain through a fine-mesh sieve into a bowl. Add the vanilla and stir to combine.

Place the bowl in a larger bowl partially filled with ice cubes and water. Stir occasionally until cool. Cover with plastic wrap, pressing it directly on the surface of the custard to prevent a skin from forming. Refrigerate until chilled, at least 3 hours or up to 24 hours.

Pour the custard into an ice-cream maker and freeze according to the manufacturer's instructions. When nearly frozen and the consistency of thick whipped cream, stir in the chocolate chunks, walnuts, and marshmallows. Transfer the ice cream to a freezer-safe container. Cover and freeze until firm, at least 3 hours or up to 3 days, before serving.

MAKES ABOUT 1 QUART (32 FL OZ/1 L)

MARSHMALLOWS

Legend has it that William Dreyer, one of the founders of Dreyer's Grand Ice Cream in the United States, created rocky road ice cream in 1929 to try to lift the country's spirits after the stock market crashed. The original recipe contained nuts and, equally as important, bite-sized pieces of marshmallow. These soft, white pillows of sweetness are made primarily from corn syrup and gelatin, although at one time they were made from the root of the marshmallow plant. Mini-marshmallows, about ½ inch (12 mm) across, are sold in a variety of pastel colors, but white is best for this recipe.

1½ cups (12 fl oz/375 ml) whole milk

1½ cups (12 fl oz/375 ml) heavy (double) cream

6 oz (185 g) bittersweet or semisweet (plain) chocolate, coarsely chopped, plus 2 oz (60 g), cut into ½-inch (12-mm) chunks

4 large egg yolks

½ cup (4 oz/125 g) sugar

Pinch of salt

1 teaspoon vanilla extract (essence)

¼ cup (1 oz/30 g) coarsely chopped walnuts

¼ cup (½ oz/15 g) mini-marshmallows

WHITE CHOCOLATE ICE CREAM

1½ cups (12 fl oz/375 ml) whole milk

1 cup (8 fl oz/250 ml) heavy (double) cream

4 oz (125 g) white chocolate, coarsely chopped

4 large egg yolks

½ cup (4 oz/125 g) sugar

Pinch of salt

In a heavy 2-qt (2-l) saucepan, combine the milk and ½ cup (4 fl oz/125 ml) of the cream. Cook over medium heat until bubbles form around the edges of the pan, about 5 minutes.

Put the chopped white chocolate in a heatproof bowl. Pour the hot milk mixture over the chocolate and let stand until melted, about 3 minutes. (Set the saucepan aside for later use.) Whisk until the mixture is smooth.

Meanwhile, in a separate bowl, combine the egg yolks, sugar, salt, and remaining ½ cup (4 fl oz/125 ml) cream. Whisk until the mixture is smooth and the sugar begins to dissolve.

Gradually whisk about ½ cup (4 fl oz/125 ml) of the warm milk mixture into the egg mixture, whisking constantly, until smooth. Pour the egg mixture into the reserved saucepan and stir in the remaining milk mixture. Cook over medium heat, stirring constantly with a wooden spoon and keeping the custard at a low simmer, until it is thick enough to coat the back of the spoon and leaves a clear trail when a finger is drawn through it, 4–6 minutes. Do not let the custard boil. Strain through a fine-mesh sieve into a bowl.

Place the bowl in a larger bowl partially filled with ice cubes and water. Stir occasionally until cool. Cover with plastic wrap, pressing it directly on the surface of the custard to prevent a skin from forming. Refrigerate until chilled, at least 3 hours or up to 24 hours.

Pour the custard into an ice-cream maker and freeze according to the manufacturer's instructions. Transfer the ice cream to a freezer-safe container. Cover and freeze until firm, at least 3 hours or up to 3 days, before serving.

MAKES ABOUT 1 QUART (32 FL OZ/1 L)

WHITE CHOCOLATE

Despite its name, white chocolate is nothing more than cocoa butter, sugar, and milk solids. It does not contain cocoa or chocolate liquor, which explains its ivory color. Choose the brand you prefer from any number of high-quality chocolate manufacturers such as Lindt, Callebaut, or Valrhona. White chocolate will not melt as easily as dark chocolate; as it is stirred, however, it will smooth out. Do not confuse white chocolate with a similar product called confectionery coating, which is bright white and made with vegetable fat flavored to taste like chocolate.

CARAMEL ICE CREAM

In a heavy 2-qt (2-l) saucepan, combine the ¾ cup (6 oz/185 g) sugar, the water, and the lemon juice. Cook over medium-high heat, stirring with a wooden spoon until the sugar dissolves, 1–2 minutes. Stop stirring at this point and cook until the syrup is amber, 5–6 minutes, swirling it to ensure even cooking. Watch closely to avoid burning. If it does burn, discard it and start again.

Remove the pan from the heat. Using oven mitts to protect your hands and arms, pour ¾ cup (6 fl oz/180 ml) of the cream into the hot syrup, taking care so it does not splash. Stir with a long-handled wooden spoon until smooth. Place over medium heat and cook until bubbles form around the edges of the pan, about 5 minutes. Remove from the heat, cover, and set aside.

Meanwhile, combine the egg yolks, salt, the 2 tablespoons sugar, and the remaining ¼ cup (2 fl oz/60 ml) cream in a bowl. Whisk until smooth. Stir in the milk.

Pour the milk mixture into the warm caramel and cook over medium heat, stirring constantly with a wooden spoon and keeping the custard at a low simmer, until it is thick enough to coat the back of the spoon and leaves a clear trail when a finger is drawn through it, 4–6 minutes. Do not let the custard boil. Strain through a fine-mesh sieve into a bowl. Stir in the vanilla.

Place the bowl in a larger bowl partially filled with ice cubes and water. Stir occasionally until cool. Cover with plastic wrap, pressing it directly on the surface of the custard to prevent a skin from forming. Refrigerate until chilled, at least 3 hours or up to 24 hours.

Pour the custard into an ice-cream maker and freeze according to the manufacturer's instructions. Transfer the ice cream to a freezer-safe container. Cover and freeze until firm, at least 3 hours or up to 3 days, before serving. Serve drizzled with the sauce.

MAKES ABOUT 1 QUART (32 FL OZ/1 L)

Ingredients (sidebar):

¾ cup (6 oz/185 g) sugar, plus 2 tablespoons

2 tablespoons water

½ teaspoon fresh lemon juice

1 cup (8 fl oz/240 ml) heavy (double) cream

4 large egg yolks

Pinch of salt

1½ cups (12 fl oz/375 ml) whole milk

1 tablespoon vanilla extract (essence)

Chocolate Sauce (page 112)

CARAMELIZING SUGAR

As sugar caramelizes, its flavor becomes less sweet and more complex. It also gets extremely hot. Sugar is considered caramelized when it reaches 320°F (160°C) to 350°F (180°C) on a candy thermometer. At these temperatures, it can cause serious burns. Be sure to use pot holders, heavy pans, and wooden utensils, which do not conduct heat. You cannot rush caramelizing, but once the sugar turns amber, it can cross the line from caramelized sugar to burned sugar in an instant. Watch it carefully.

PUMPKIN ICE CREAM

1 cup (8 oz/250 g) fresh pumpkin purée *(far right)* or canned unsweetened pumpkin purée

1 teaspoon vanilla extract (essence)

2 cups (16 fl oz/500 ml) heavy (double) cream

¾ cup (6 oz/185 g) firmly packed dark brown sugar

5 large egg yolks

½ teaspoon ground cinnamon

½ teaspoon ground ginger

¼ teaspoon salt

Pinch of freshly grated nutmeg

1 tablespoon bourbon

In a bowl, whisk the pumpkin purée and vanilla together. Cover and chill for at least 3 hours or up to 8 hours.

In a heavy 2-qt (2-l) saucepan, combine 1½ cups (12 fl oz/375 ml) of the cream and ½ cup (4 oz/125 g) of the brown sugar. Cook over medium heat until bubbles form around the edges of the pan, about 5 minutes.

Meanwhile, combine the egg yolks, cinnamon, ginger, salt, nutmeg, remaining ½ cup (4 fl oz/125 ml) cream, and remaining ¼ cup (2 oz/60 g) brown sugar in a bowl. Whisk until the mixture is smooth and the sugar begins to dissolve.

Remove the cream mixture from the heat. Gradually whisk about ½ cup (4 fl oz/125 ml) of the hot cream mixture into the egg mixture, whisking constantly, until smooth. Pour the egg mixture into the saucepan. Cook over medium heat, stirring constantly with a wooden spoon and keeping the custard at a low simmer, until it is thick enough to coat the back of the spoon and leaves a clear trail when a finger is drawn through it, 4–6 minutes. Do not let the custard boil. Strain through a fine-mesh sieve into a bowl.

Place the bowl in a larger bowl partially filled with ice cubes and water. Stir occasionally until cool. Whisk the pumpkin mixture into the custard. Cover with plastic wrap, pressing it directly on the surface of the custard to prevent a skin from forming. Refrigerate until chilled, at least 3 hours or up to 24 hours.

Pour the custard into an ice-cream maker and freeze according to the manufacturer's instructions. Add the bourbon during the last minute of churning. Transfer the ice cream to a freezer-safe container. Cover and freeze until firm, at least 3 hours or up to 3 days, before serving.

MAKES ABOUT 1 QUART (32 FL OZ/1 L)

PUMPKIN PURÉE

To make your own pumpkin purée, use 1 large or 2 medium Sugar Pie or other eating (not field) pumpkins. Cut out the stem and quarter the pumpkin lengthwise. In a preheated 400°F (200°C) oven, bake the quarters, cut side down, in a shallow roasting pan with a little water in the bottom until tender, about 1 hour. Let cool, scrape out the seeds, cut the flesh from the peels, and force it through a medium-mesh sieve or the medium disk of a food mill. Freeze any leftover purée for up to 2 months.

CHOCOLATE FUDGE SWIRL ICE CREAM

FUDGE SAUCE

Combine ⅔ cup (5 fl oz/160 ml) heavy (double) cream, ½ cup (5 oz/155 g) light corn syrup, and 2 tablespoons firmly packed dark brown sugar in a heavy saucepan. Bring to a boil over medium-low heat, stirring occasionally until the sugar dissolves, about 5 minutes. In a bowl, combine 5 oz (155 g) bittersweet or semisweet (plain) chocolate, coarsely chopped, and a pinch of salt. Pour the hot cream mixture over the chocolate and stir until melted and smooth. Add 1 teaspoon vanilla extract (essence) and stir to combine. Makes about 1 cup (8 fl oz/250 ml).

Prepare the fudge sauce as directed *(left)*. Set aside and let cool to room temperature. When cool, remove a generous ⅔ cup (5 fl oz/160 ml). Cover and refrigerate the remaining fudge for another use.

In a heavy 2-qt (2-l) saucepan, combine the half-and-half, cream, sugar, and salt. Cook over medium heat until bubbles form around the edges of the pan, about 5 minutes.

Meanwhile, combine the bittersweet and milk chocolates in a heatproof bowl. Pour the hot cream mixture over and stir until the chocolates melt and the mixture is smooth. Strain the cream mixture through a fine-mesh sieve into a bowl. Add the vanilla and stir to combine.

Place the bowl in a larger bowl partially filled with ice cubes and water. Stir occasionally until cool. Cover with plastic wrap, pressing it directly on the surface of the cream mixture to prevent a skin from forming. Refrigerate for at least 3 hours or up to 24 hours.

Pour the cream mixture into an ice-cream maker and freeze according to the manufacturer's instructions. Spoon about one-fourth of the ice cream into a 1.5-qt (48–fl oz/1.5-l) freezer-safe container, or use 2 smaller containers. Whisk the fudge sauce to loosen it. Spoon a layer of the fudge sauce evenly over the ice cream and top with another layer of ice cream. Continue to layer the ice cream and fudge sauce in the same way, ending with a layer of ice cream.

Cover and freeze until firm, at least 3 hours or up to 3 days, before serving. As you scoop down into the ice cream, the layers of fudge will appear as a swirl.

MAKES ABOUT 1¼ QUARTS (40 FL OZ/1 L)

Fudge Sauce *(far left)*

2 cups (16 fl oz/500 ml) half-and-half (half cream)

1 cup (8 fl oz/250 ml) heavy (double) cream

⅓ cup (3 oz/90 g) sugar

Pinch of salt

4 oz (125 g) bittersweet or semisweet (plain) chocolate, finely chopped

2 oz (60 g) milk chocolate, finely chopped

1½ teaspoons vanilla extract (essence)

CRÈME FRAÎCHE ICE CREAM WITH CANDIED LEMON ZEST

1½ cups (12 fl oz/375 ml) half-and-half (half cream)

1 vanilla bean, split lengthwise

4 large egg yolks

½ cup (4 oz/125 g) plus 2 tablespoons sugar

Pinch of salt

1½ cups (12 oz/375 g) crème fraîche *(far right)*, chilled

¼ cup (1 oz/30 g) Candied Lemon Zest (page 113)

In a heavy 2-qt (2-l) saucepan, heat 1 cup (8 fl oz/250 ml) of the half-and-half over medium heat. Using the tip of a sharp knife, scrape the seeds from the vanilla bean into the half-and-half and then add the vanilla bean. Cook until bubbles form around the edges of the pan, about 5 minutes.

Meanwhile, combine the egg yolks, sugar, salt, and remaining ½ cup (4 fl oz/125 ml) half-and-half in a bowl. Whisk until the mixture is smooth and the sugar begins to dissolve.

Remove the half-and-half from the heat. Gradually whisk about ½ cup (4 fl oz/125 ml) of the hot half-and-half into the egg mixture, whisking constantly, until smooth. Pour the egg mixture into the saucepan. Cook over medium heat, stirring constantly with a wooden spoon and keeping the custard at a low simmer, until it is thick enough to coat the back of the spoon and leaves a clear trail when a finger is drawn through it, 4–6 minutes. Do not let the custard boil. Strain through a fine-mesh sieve into a bowl. Discard the vanilla bean.

Place the bowl in a larger bowl partially filled with ice cubes and water. Stir occasionally until cool. Cover with plastic wrap, pressing it directly on the surface of the custard to prevent a skin from forming. Refrigerate until chilled, at least 3 hours or up to 24 hours.

Whisk the crème fraîche into the custard. Pour the custard into an ice-cream maker and freeze according to the manufacturer's instructions. When nearly frozen and the consistency of thick whipped cream, add the candied zest. Churn or stir just until mixed. Transfer the ice cream to a freezer-safe container. Cover and freeze until firm, at least 3 hours or up to 3 days, before serving.

MAKES ABOUT 1 QUART (32 FL OZ/1 L)

CRÈME FRAÎCHE

Originally from France, crème fraîche is similar to sour cream but sweeter and milder, with a hint of nuttiness. It may be purchased, or you can make your own. Combine 1½ cups (12 fl oz/375 ml) heavy (double) cream and 1½ tablespoons buttermilk in a small saucepan over medium-low heat. Heat to lukewarm, but do not allow to simmer. Remove from the heat, cover, and allow to thicken at warm room temperature until it is as thick and flavorful as you want it, 8–48 hours. Makes 1½ cups (12 oz/375 g).

ZABAGLIONE GELATO

ZABAGLIONE

Zabaglione is a greatly admired, thickened custard that originated in Italy and is defined by the addition of wine, usually sweet Marsala. Other wines can be used, such as sherry, a fortified wine that home cooks are more likely to have on hand. In France, a similar custard is called sabayon. In both countries, the custard is served as a dessert in stemmed glasses or as an especially rich sauce. It is delicious spooned over sweet puddings, warm apple or pear tarts, sliced fresh fruit, and plain cakes.

To make the zabaglione, whisk together the Marsala, sugar, egg yolks, and salt in the top of a double boiler (page 114) and set over barely simmering water. Cook the mixture over medium-low heat, whisking constantly, until foamy and thickened enough to fall in a slowly dissolving ribbon when the whisk is lifted, 5–7 minutes. Place the top of the double boiler in a large bowl partially filled with ice cubes and water. Stir occasionally until cool. Cover with plastic wrap, pressing it directly on the surface. Refrigerate until chilled, at least 3 hours or up to 24 hours.

In a heavy 2-qt (2-l) saucepan, combine the milk and ½ cup (4 fl oz/ 125 ml) of the cream. Cook over medium heat until bubbles form around the edges of the pan, about 5 minutes.

Meanwhile, combine the egg yolks, sugar, salt, and remaining ½ cup (4 fl oz/125 ml) cream in a bowl. Whisk until smooth. Remove the milk mixture from the heat. Gradually whisk about ½ cup (4 fl oz/125 ml) of the hot milk mixture into the egg mixture until smooth. Pour the egg mixture into the pan. Cook over medium heat at a low simmer, stirring constantly, until it is thick enough to coat the back of a spoon and leaves a clear trail when a finger is drawn through it, 4–6 minutes. Do not let boil. Strain through a fine-mesh sieve into a bowl. Stir in the vanilla.

Place the bowl in a larger bowl partially filled with ice cubes and water. Stir occasionally until cool. Cover with plastic wrap, pressing it on the surface. Refrigerate for at least 3 hours or up to 24 hours.

Pour the custard into an ice-cream maker and freeze according to the manufacturer's instructions. When nearly frozen and the consistency of thick whipped cream, churn or stir in the zabaglione. Transfer the ice cream to a freezer-safe container. Freeze until firm, at least 3 hours or up to 3 days, before serving.

MAKES ABOUT 1 QUART (32 FL OZ/1 L)

FOR THE ZABAGLIONE:

¼ cup (2 fl oz/60 ml) Marsala or medium-dry sherry

¼ cup (2 oz/60 g) sugar

3 large egg yolks

Pinch of salt

2 cups (16 fl oz/500 ml) whole milk

1 cup (8 fl oz/250 ml) heavy (double) cream

3 large egg yolks

¼ cup (2 oz/60 g) sugar

Pinch of salt

¼ teaspoon vanilla extract (essence)

CHOCOLATE-RASPBERRY TRUFFLE ICE CREAM

In a heavy 2-qt (2-l) saucepan, combine 1 cup (8 fl oz/250 ml) of the cream and the milk. Cook over medium heat until bubbles form around the edges of the pan, about 5 minutes.

Put the chopped chocolate in a heatproof bowl. Pour the hot cream mixture over the chocolate and let stand until melted, about 3 minutes. (Set the saucepan aside for later use.) Whisk until the mixture is smooth.

Meanwhile, combine the egg yolks, sugar, and remaining ½ cup (4 fl oz/125 ml) cream in a bowl. Whisk until the mixture is smooth and the sugar begins to dissolve.

Gradually whisk about ½ cup (4 fl oz/125 ml) of the warm cream mixture into the egg mixture, whisking constantly, until smooth. Pour the egg mixture into the reserved saucepan and stir in the remaining cream mixture. Cook over medium heat, stirring constantly with a wooden spoon and keeping the custard at a low simmer, until it is thick enough to coat the back of the spoon and leaves a clear trail when a finger is drawn through it, 4–6 minutes. Do not let the custard boil. Strain through a fine-mesh sieve into a bowl. Add the vanilla and stir to combine.

Place the bowl in a larger bowl partially filled with ice cubes and water. Stir occasionally until cool. Cover with plastic wrap, pressing it directly on the surface of the custard to prevent a skin from forming. Refrigerate until chilled, at least 3 hours or up to 24 hours.

Meanwhile, make the ganache: In a small saucepan, heat the cream and butter over medium heat until the butter melts and bubbles form around the edges of the pan, about 3 minutes.

Put the chopped chocolate in a heatproof bowl. Pour the hot cream mixture over the chocolate and let stand until melted, about 3 minutes. Whisk until the mixture is smooth. Add the Chambord and stir to combine. Pour the truffle mixture into

1½ cups (12 fl oz/375 ml) heavy (double) cream

1 cup (8 fl oz/250 ml) whole milk

4 oz (125 g) bittersweet or semisweet (plain) chocolate, coarsely chopped

4 large egg yolks

½ cup (4 oz/125 g) sugar

1 teaspoon vanilla extract (essence)

FOR THE GANACHE:

¼ cup (2 fl oz/60 ml) heavy (double) cream

1 tablespoon unsalted butter

4 oz (125 g) bittersweet or semisweet (plain) chocolate, coarsely chopped

1 tablespoon Chambord liqueur

FOR THE RASPBERRY SWIRL:

⅓ cup (3 oz/90 g) seedless raspberry jam or preserves

2 tablespoons Chambord liqueur

a lightly greased, small, shallow pan or dish. Let cool to room temperature, cover, and refrigerate until ready to use.

Shortly before freezing the ice cream, make the raspberry swirl: In a small saucepan, combine the jam and Chambord. Warm gently over low heat, stirring to blend, about 3 minutes. Remove from the heat and let cool completely.

Pour the chocolate custard into an ice-cream maker and freeze according to the manufacturer's instructions.

Meanwhile, remove the truffle mixture from the refrigerator and let it soften slightly. Using your fingers or a small knife, break the mixture into small pieces.

When the ice cream is nearly frozen and the consistency of thick whipped cream, add the truffle pieces. Churn or stir just until mixed. Spoon about one-fourth of the ice cream into a 1.5-qt (48–fl oz/1.5-l) freezer-safe container, or use 2 smaller containers. Spoon a layer of raspberry swirl evenly over the ice cream and top with another layer of ice cream. Continue to layer the ice cream and raspberry swirl in the same way, ending with a layer of ice cream.

Freeze for at least 3 hours before serving. As you scoop down into the ice cream, the layers of raspberry will appear as a swirl.

MAKES ABOUT 1 QUART (32 FL OZ/1 L)

(Photograph appears on following page.)

TRUFFLES

Truffles are made from ganache, which, in its purest form, is a mixture of cream and high-quality bittersweet or semisweet (plain) chocolate. It may also include butter. To make the truffles found in fine chocolate shops and gourmet food stores, ganache is most commonly rolled into balls and then dipped in chocolate or rolled in cocoa powder or sugar. The ganache may be flavored with a wide array of ingredients, from liqueurs to hazelnuts (filberts) to lemon zest. In this recipe, ganache is chilled and then broken into coarse pieces.

ICE CREAM DISHES

A bowl or waffle cone filled with unadorned ice cream is simple and delicious, but a more elaborate dish, such as a sundae, sandwich, or terrine, is sublime. Mix and match your favorite sauces, cookies, fruits, and nuts with your favorite ice creams to make delightful creations that are sure to both satisfy your appetite and appeal to your sense of culinary adventure.

HOT FUDGE SUNDAE WITH STRAWBERRIES

Reserve 6 of the best strawberries for garnish. Hull the rest and slice thickly lengthwise. Put the sliced berries in a bowl and sprinkle with the sugar to taste, depending on the sweetness of the berries. Toss to combine. Cover and set aside at room temperature for up to 1 hour, or refrigerate for up to 4 hours.

Prepare the fudge sauce as directed on page 82 (see Note).

Spoon about 1 tablespoon of the fudge sauce into 6 individual sundae dishes or dessert bowls. Top with large scoops of ice cream, 2–3 tablespoons of the fudge sauce, and a generous serving of the strawberries. Spoon whipped cream on top. Garnish each sundae with a reserved strawberry.

Note: You must use the fudge sauce while it's still hot to have a true hot fudge sundae. But this doesn't mean you can't prepare the sauce in advance. After it has cooled, the sauce may be covered and refrigerated for up to 3 days. Reheat it in a bowl set over a saucepan partially filled with simmering water, stirring until the sauce is hot.

MAKES 6 SERVINGS

2 cups (8 oz/250 g) fresh strawberries

1–2 tablespoons sugar

1 cup (8 fl oz/250 ml) Fudge Sauce (page 82)

1 qt (32 fl oz/1 l) Vanilla Bean Ice Cream (page 10), Espresso Ice Cream with Dark Chocolate Chunks (page 53), or Strawberry Ice Cream (page 17)

Sweetened Whipped Cream (page 42)

SUNDAE VARIATIONS

Only your imagination and the ice cream flavors in the freezer limit the variety of sundaes you can make. Vanilla topped with sauce, whipped cream, and other fixings most often defines a sundae, but there is no reason not to use other ice cream flavors such as Country Peach ((page 29), Double-Chocolate (page 13), or Ginger (page 62). After the hot fudge sundae, perhaps the best known is the banana split: one scoop each of vanilla, chocolate, and strawberry ice cream on a split banana, drizzled with butterscotch, chocolate, and marshmallow sauces, and topped with whipped cream and cherries.

ICE CREAM SANDWICHES

FOR THE CHOCOLATE
COOKIES:

1¼ cups (9 oz/280 g)
firmly packed dark brown
sugar

½ cup (4 oz/125 g)
unsalted butter

3 oz (90 g) unsweetened
chocolate, coarsely
chopped

1 large egg

2 teaspoons vanilla extract
(essence)

1¼ cups (6½ oz/200 g)
all-purpose (plain) flour

¾ teaspoon baking soda
(bicarbonate of soda)

¼ teaspoon salt

1½ cups (9 oz/280 g)
semisweet (plain)
chocolate chips

2 cups (16 fl oz/500 ml)
Raspberry Ice Cream
(page 65), Mint–Chocolate
Chip Ice Cream (page 18),
or other ice cream of
choice, slightly softened

To make the cookies, preheat the oven to 350°F (180°C). Lightly grease 2 baking sheets.

In a heavy saucepan, combine the brown sugar, butter, and chopped chocolate. Cook over low heat, stirring frequently, until the chocolate melts (the mixture will look grainy). Transfer to a bowl and let cool to lukewarm.

Add the egg and vanilla to the chocolate mixture and whisk until smooth. In another bowl, whisk the flour, baking soda, and salt together. Add the dry ingredients to the chocolate mixture and stir until blended. Stir in the chocolate chips. Cover and refrigerate until firm enough to form into cookies, about 30 minutes.

Drop the cookie dough by generous tablespoons onto the prepared baking sheets. Dampen your fingers with cold water and smooth the cookies into slightly flattened rounds about 3 inches (7.5 cm) in diameter. Space the cookies at least 1½ inches (4 cm) apart. You should have 8 cookies.

Bake the cookies until the edges darken and the centers are still slightly soft, 10–12 minutes. Transfer the cookies to wire racks to cool completely.

To assemble the sandwiches, lay 4 of the cookies, flat side up, on a work surface. Spread about ½ cup (4 fl oz/125 ml) of the ice cream on each cookie. Top each with one of the remaining cookies, flat side down. Smooth the sides and wrap each sandwich in plastic wrap. Lay on clean, dry baking sheets and freeze until firm, at least 2 hours or up to 3 days.

MAKES 4 SANDWICHES

ICE CREAM SANDWICH VARIATIONS

The large, chewy double-chocolate cookies in this recipe are perfect for ice cream sandwiches, but chocolate chip cookies may also be used. Bake your favorite recipe, but halve the amount of chips. Do not let the cookies sit on the baking sheets for more than 2–3 minutes after removing them from the oven, or they will stick. Slip a spatula under the cookies and transfer them to wire racks to cool completely. Other ice cream flavors that make terrific sandwiches include Chocolate Fudge Swirl (page 82) and Pistachio and Dried Cherry (page 49).

PEACH AND DARK RUM ICE CREAM TORTE

RUM

A spirit that originated in the Caribbean, rum is distilled from sugarcane juice or molasses. This slightly sweet liquor is especially well suited for mixed drinks and desserts.

The darker the rum, the stronger its flavor, but if you have only light or white rum in your cupboard, it will work in this torte. As for other spirits, the alcohol content of rum is designated by its proof, which is always twice the percentage of alcohol. For example, 80 proof rum is 40 percent alcohol.

Preheat the oven to 350°F (180°C). Line an 8-inch (20-cm) springform pan with plastic wrap, leaving a 6-inch (15-cm) overhang all around. In a food processor, pulse 9 of the ladyfingers to fine crumbs. Spread the crumbs on a baking sheet and toast in the oven, stirring once or twice, until lightly browned and fragrant, 4–5 minutes. Slide the crumbs onto a plate and set aside to cool.

Arrange some of the remaining ladyfingers in the springform pan so that they stand upright, rounded sides facing out, around the sides of the pan, fitting them snugly. Cover the bottom of the springform pan with the remaining ladyfingers, trimming them as necessary to fit. Reserve 3 tablespoons of the rum and generously brush the remaining rum over the ladyfingers in the pan to saturate them.

Spoon the peach ice cream into the springform pan and spread it in an even layer. Sprinkle evenly with all but 2–3 tablespoons of the toasted ladyfinger crumbs. Drizzle the remaining 3 tablespoons rum over the crumbs in the pan. Spoon the crème fraîche ice cream into the pan and spread it in an even layer. Sprinkle the remaining ladyfinger crumbs decoratively around the outside edge of the torte, using a stencil to create a scallop pattern if desired.

Pull the overhanging plastic wrap up and over the torte. Freeze until firm, at least 3 hours or up to overnight.

To serve, remove the sides of the springform pan, peel away the plastic wrap, garnish with the peach and lemon slices (if using), and cut the torte into wedges.

Note: This recipe was designed for use with 3-inch (7.5-cm), spongecake-style ladyfingers, commonly found in most supermarkets. If you use longer, crisper Italian ladyfingers, you will need to add another cup of each type of ice cream listed above.

MAKES 8–10 SERVINGS

32–38 ladyfingers

½ cup (4 fl oz/125 ml) dark rum

3 cups (24 fl oz/750 ml) Country Peach Ice Cream (page 29), slightly softened

3 cups (24 fl oz/750 ml) Crème Fraîche Ice Cream with Candied Lemon Zest (page 85), slightly softened

Peach slices for garnish (optional)

Lemon slices for garnish (optional)

MAPLE-WALNUT PARFAIT

4 large egg yolks

½ cup (5½ fl oz/170 ml) pure maple syrup

Pinch of salt

1 cup (8 fl oz/250 ml) heavy (double) cream

¾ cup (3 oz/90 g) Sugared Walnuts *(far right)*, crushed, plus 4–8 halves for serving

Sweetened Whipped Cream for serving (page 42)

In the top of a double boiler (page 114) set over barely simmering water, whisk together the egg yolks, maple syrup, and salt until the mixture is thick enough to fall in a slowly dissolving ribbon when the whisk is lifted, 6–8 minutes. Remove the top pan from the heat and set aside to cool to room temperature, about 15 minutes.

Using an electric mixer on medium-high speed, beat the cream until soft peaks form. Fold into the cooled egg-maple mixture. Scrape into an 8-inch (20-cm) square pan, cover with plastic wrap or aluminum foil, and freeze until firm, at least 3 hours or up to overnight.

Just before serving, stir the frozen maple cream to soften it.

Put about 1 tablespoon of the crushed walnuts into each of 4 stemmed dessert dishes or small glass bowls. Scoop about ¼ cup (2 oz/60 g) of the maple cream into each dish. Repeat layering with the walnuts to make 3 layers. Top each parfait with 1 or 2 sugared walnut halves and whipped cream. Serve at once.

Note: Meaning "perfect" in French, a parfait *was originally a simple dessert consisting of small scoops of sweet iced coffee cream. The scoops might be presented in tall, slender glasses or on pretty plates. Soon other flavors of ices and frozen custards were served as parfaits, and in America, the dessert evolved into a layered dessert made with ice cream, syrup, and whipped cream. This maple parfait is true to the original intent of a frozen flavored custard served simply.*

MAKES 4 SERVINGS

SUGARED WALNUTS

Preheat the oven to 350°F (180°C). In a bowl, toss together 2 cups (8 oz/250 g) walnut halves, 3 tablespoons sugar, and ¼ teaspoon salt. Spread in a single layer in a roasting pan. Scatter 2½ tablespoons unsalted butter, cut into pieces, over the nuts and stir gently to mix. Roast, stirring the nuts and shaking the pan several times, until lightly browned, 10–12 minutes. For darker nuts, roast 2–3 minutes longer. Spread the nuts out onto a large platter or baking sheet to cool. Use at once, or store in an airtight container at room temperature for up to 3 days. Makes about 2 cups (8 oz/250 g).

WHITE AND DARK CHOCOLATE TERRINE
WITH RASPBERRY SAUCE

TERRINE VARIATIONS
The term *terrine* applies to a type of recipe as well as the rectangular loaf pan in which it is made. Other cookies and ice creams may be substituted for the ones used in this recipe. Use gingersnap crumbs with Ginger Ice Cream (page 62) and Pumpkin Ice Cream (page 81), for example, or crush vanilla or chocolate wafers and layer them with Meyer Lemon Sorbet (page 22) and Tangerine Sorbet (page 69). Amaretti crumbs in a terrine with Amaretto Ice Cream (page 61) and Caramel Ice Cream (page 78) is another delicious choice.

Line a 4-by-8-inch (10-by-20-cm) loaf pan with plastic wrap, leaving a 6-inch (15-cm) overhang on both of the long sides.

Put the cookies in a 1-gallon (4-l) zippered, heavy-duty plastic bag. Lay the bag on a work surface and roll a rolling pin over it until the cookies are crushed to fine crumbs. (Do not make the crumbs in a food processor or blender; they will be too fine.) You should have about 1½ cups (4½ oz/140 g) coarse crumbs.

To assemble the terrine, spoon half of the Chocolate-Raspberry Truffle Ice Cream into the pan and spread it in an even layer. Sprinkle evenly with one-third of the cookie crumbs. Next, spoon the White Chocolate Ice Cream into the pan and spread it evenly over the crumbs. Sprinkle with half of the remaining cookie crumbs. Finally, spoon the remaining Chocolate-Raspberry Truffle Ice Cream into the pan and spread it evenly over the crumbs to cover completely. Sprinkle with the remaining crumbs, pressing them into the ice cream so that they adhere.

Pull the overhanging plastic wrap up and over the ice cream to cover. Freeze for at least 3 hours or up to overnight.

To serve, unfold the plastic. Let the terrine sit at room temperature for 3–5 minutes, depending on the heat of the kitchen. Invert a plate over the terrine and, holding the plate firmly on the pan, invert them together. Gently lift the pan off the terrine and peel off the plastic. If the pan does not lift off easily, wrap the bottom of the pan with a well-wrung, damp warm kitchen towel for 30 seconds.

Cut the terrine into slices and serve with the raspberry sauce.

MAKES 8-10 SERVINGS

35–40 chocolate wafer cookies, broken into pieces

3 cups (24 fl oz/750 ml) Chocolate-Raspberry Truffle Ice Cream (page 88), slightly softened

1 cup (8 fl oz/250 ml) White Chocolate Ice Cream (page 77), slightly softened

2 cups (16 fl oz/500 ml) Raspberry Sauce (page 113)

INDIVIDUAL BAKED ALASKAS

¼ cup (2 fl oz/60 ml) water

¾ cup (6 oz/185 g) sugar

6 slices purchased almond or plain pound cake, each ½ inch (12 mm) thick

2 cups (16 fl oz/500 ml) Vanilla Bean Ice Cream (page 10), Double-Chocolate Ice Cream (page 13), or Pistachio and Dried Cherry Ice Cream (page 49), slightly softened

3 large egg whites

¼ teaspoon cream of tartar

In a small, heavy saucepan, combine the water and ¼ cup (2 oz/ 60 g) of the sugar. Bring to a boil over medium-high heat and cook, stirring occasionally, until the sugar dissolves and the syrup is clear, about 1 minute. Set aside to cool to room temperature.

Arrange six 6–fl oz (180-ml) custard cups on a work surface. Trim each pound cake slice so that it fits into a cup and reserve the trimmings. (The slices must cover the bottoms fully). Using your fingers, crumble the trimmings into coarse crumbs.

Brush the cake layers with the cooled syrup. Spoon about ⅓ cup (3 fl oz/80 ml) ice cream into each custard cup, and press firmly to cover the cake and fill the cup. Smooth the top and sprinkle with cake crumbs, then press to adhere. Set the cups on a baking sheet, cover, and freeze until firm, at least 3 hours or up to overnight.

Preheat the oven to 450°F (230°C).

Using an electric mixer on medium speed or a wire whisk, beat the egg whites until foamy. Add the cream of tartar and continue to beat on medium-high speed until soft peaks form. Gradually beat in the remaining ½ cup (4 oz/125 g) sugar and continue beating until stiff, glossy peaks form. Remove the cups from the freezer. Spoon the meringue over the top of each cup, covering the top completely and swirling the meringue into a high dome.

Return the custard cups to the baking sheet and bake until the meringue is lightly browned, 2–3 minutes. Serve at once.

Note: This recipe contains partially cooked egg whites. For more information, see page 114.

MAKES 6 SERVINGS

BEATING EGG WHITES

Begin with a spotlessly clean copper or stainless-steel bowl and clean, dry beaters when beating egg whites. The whites will not expand if even a speck of egg yolk or any other fat is present. Use an electric mixer or wire whisk to beat them; food processors and blenders will not aerate the whites properly. Adding a little cream of tartar to the whites while they are still frothy helps stabilize them. For stiff peaks, the opaque white foam should stand in obvious peaks when the beaters are lifted.

ICE CREAM BASICS

There is something about the cold sweetness of ice cream melting on our tongues that comforts and soothes us as few other foods do. Children stop crying and adults smile with anticipation when offered this irresistible treat. Like freshly baked bread or a pie made from scratch, homemade ice cream is well worth the time it takes to make a batch.

EQUIPMENT

Unlike the hand-cranked ice-cream machines of the past, today's ice-cream machines are easy to use, are relatively inexpensive, and work quickly, which means you can have a fresh batch of ice cream in as little as 20 minutes once you flip the switch.

The most common ice-cream machines for home kitchens are electrically powered. Most contain a canister with sides that are filled with coolant. These machines do not need ice. The coolant is liquid at room temperature, but turns hard and very cold when frozen. Once the frozen canister is locked into the outer shell of the ice-cream machine and the dasher is inserted, it is cold enough to freeze the chilled custard or other mixture in a short period of time.

The only downsides to these machines are that you need to plan ahead—the canisters require at least 6 hours in the freezer—and you won't be able to make more than about a quart (1 l) at one time, enough for 6 to 8 servings. You can keep a canister in the freezer at all times or buy 2 canisters, but this may take up valuable room in your freezer.

Some folks still prefer the old-fashioned, hand-cranked machines that require you to pack ice chips and rock salt (which prevents the ice from melting too quickly) around the inner canister and then to turn a crank. Once in motion, the crank rotates the canister or the dasher, thus aerating the ice cream inside. These old-style machines are still available, although they are increasingly hard to find with each passing year—particularly if you want a wooden canister (most are stainless steel). These workhorses are capable of churning up to 3 to 4 quarts (3–4 l) of ice cream at a time—plenty for a crowd.

This same old-fashioned style is available in electric models, but they still require chips of ice layered with salt. Ordinary table salt will do,

however, as electric-powered machines work more quickly.

If you use a hand-cranked or electric old-fashioned machine, be sure to remove the canister from the ice and salt and wipe it clean before you scoop the ice cream into containers for further freezing. Otherwise, the melting briny ice may seep into the ice cream. Also, after using one of these machines, be sure to rinse it well to prevent the salt from corroding any part of it.

Finally, if you have enough counter space, machines with self-contained refrigeration are a good choice. With the push of a button, you can churn and freeze about a quart (1 l) of ice cream in minutes. These machines are a luxury, to be sure, but if you make ice cream often, the investment may be one you'll appreciate.

ICE CREAM

The origins of ice cream, and similar iced desserts, can be traced back over a thousand years to Rome, China, and Turkey. But the evolution of ice cream as the creamy, soft-yet-firm confection that we know and love today really began in Italy in the sixteenth century and has been perfected ever since.

Ice cream is a mixture of a few essential ingredients or components, each playing a carefully balanced role. Fat from cream and milk imparts richness, smoothness, and flavor. Too much fat, however, will cause the mixture to curdle and form small lumps. Sugar sweetens and smooths ice cream. Too little sugar will result in graininess, while too much will inhibit freezing. Eggs add body and richness and help bring together fat and water. Flavorings such as fruit purées, nuts, and liqueurs all help define the taste of each ice cream. Finally, a certain amount of air must be churned into ice cream, or it will freeze solid. More air means a lighter, softer texture and easier scooping.

FRENCH-STYLE ICE CREAM

Arguably, the best-tasting ice creams are made from custard bases and are known as French style. Egg-rich custards produce unparalleled silken textures and intense, deep flavors, yielding ice creams that most people find fuller tasting and more satisfying than other styles. Examples of this type include Vanilla Bean Ice Cream (page 10), Toasted Coconut Ice Cream (page 54), and Chocolate-Raspberry Truffle Ice Cream (page 88).

PHILADELPHIA-STYLE ICE CREAMS

Ice creams made without eggs are sometimes called Philadelphia or American style. Easier to make than custard-based ice creams, they are delicious but not as rich. Examples include Coffee Ice Cream (page 14) and Strawberry Ice Cream (page 17). The texture of ice cream made with heavy cream alone will not be as fine as ice cream made with a mixture of cream and milk.

GELATO

Gelato is Italian ice cream, made with less cream than other ice creams but from an egg-rich custard base. It has a lower percentage of fat, which means the finished product is denser and not quite as rich as other ice creams. The flavor of authentic gelato tends to be especially intense, too, because of a lower amount of air incorporated during churning.

MAKING CUSTARD

Many of the ice cream recipes in this book begin with custard, a smooth, silken fusion of eggs, cream, milk, and sugar in varying proportions. While some custard desserts are baked so that they firm up, custard for ice cream is cooked on top of the stove just until the ingredients come together as a thickened, satiny sauce.

Some cooks are wary of making custards, but with a little care, they are easy. Shown opposite are the basic steps for making a custard:

1 **Scalding the milk:** In a heavy 2-qt (2-l) saucepan, combine the milk and cream. Cook over medium heat until bubbles form around the edges of the pan, about 5 minutes.

2 **Tempering the egg yolks:** Meanwhile, combine the egg yolks, sugar, and any remaining cream called for in a recipe in a bowl. Whisk until the mixture is smooth and the sugar begins to dissolve. Remove the milk mixture from the heat and, while whisking constantly, very slowly pour about ½ cup (4 fl oz/125 ml) of the hot milk mixture into the egg mixture. Whisk until smooth. (This step heats the eggs and prevents them from curdling when you pour them into the hot milk mixture.) Pour the tempered egg mixture into the saucepan.

3 **Testing the custard:** Cook over medium heat, stirring constantly with a wooden spoon and keeping the custard at a low simmer, until it is thick enough to coat the back of the spoon and leaves a clear trail when a finger is drawn through it, 4–6 minutes. Do not let the custard boil. Strain through a fine-mesh sieve into a bowl.

4 **Cooling the custard:** Place the bowl in a larger bowl partially filled with ice cubes and water. Stir occasionally until the mixture is cool. Cover with plastic wrap, pressing it directly on the surface of the custard to prevent a skin from forming. Refrigerate until chilled, at least 3 hours or up to 24 hours.

Following are tips and extra steps that you can take to help ensure success when making custard:

Use a heavy, nonaluminum saucepan to prevent scorching and cook the custard over medium to medium-low heat. If you are just beginning to make custards, you may want to reduce the heat to low to ensure that the custard cooks gently and does not scorch or curdle. As an extra precaution, cook the custard in the top of a double boiler or use a heat diffuser—a flat, heavy disk made of enameled cast iron that sits between the burner and the bottom of a pan and helps to evenly distribute heat and prevent scorching. When you become more adept at custard making, you can raise the heat to medium—but never any higher.

Stir the custard with a wooden spoon or heatproof rubber spatula. These are more efficient than metal spoons for scraping the bottom of the pan during cooking.

Be patient. Custard takes some time to thicken. If you rush, and the custard boils, the proteins in the eggs and the milk or cream will not thicken correctly, and the custard could curdle or separate.

When the custard is properly thickened, it will register between 160°F (71°C) and 170°F (77°C). You can use an instant-read thermometer to determine the temperature.

The best doneness test for custard is to wait for the custard to coat the back of the wooden spoon. Then, draw your finger along the length of the back; it should leave a clear trail. The custard will also look glossy and feel thicker as you stir.

Even the smoothest stirred custard should be strained through a fine-mesh sieve to remove lumps. This will guarantee a smooth base for a creamy finished ice cream.

You may let the custard cool on the counter, but it is a good idea to cool it quickly in an ice-water bath, especially if it is a hot day. To make an ice-water bath, use a large bowl partially filled with cold water and ice cubes. Stir the custard occasionally while it cools. It should reach room temperature in about 20 minutes. Using a stainless-steel bowl to hold the custard will also facilitate cooling, since metal conducts coolness more effectively than other materials.

When the custard reaches room temperature, lay a piece of plastic wrap directly on its surface. This will prevent a skin from forming during chilling. If a skin does form, skim it off before making the ice cream.

Refrigerate the custard for at least 3 hours so that it is very cold. Using a very cold custard will prevent ice crystals from forming when the mixture is churned. Also, the colder the custard is when added to the ice-cream maker, the more efficient the freezing process will be. The custard will keep in the refrigerator for up to 24 hours. In fact, its flavor improves as it mellows in the refrigerator. For this reason, you may want to prepare the custard base the day before you plan to make the ice cream.

SORBET, GRANITA, AND SHERBET

These frozen treats are oftentimes associated with ice cream, but they are made with little or no milk products and are lighter than custard- and cream-based ice creams. Instead, they offer a welcome burst of icy, refreshing, and often fruity flavors that few desserts can match.

SORBET

Icy and sweet, sorbets are made by incorporating air into a sweetened fruit purée or juice as it freezes in an ice-cream maker. They contain no milk, cream, or eggs. The resulting intense flavor and light texture of sorbet makes it a cool and refreshing treat—a perfect first course, palate cleanser, or light dessert. While most sorbets are made from fruit, some are made from other ingredients, including chocolate, coffee, wine, or even puréed vegetables.

GRANITA

Granita is similar to sorbet in that it is a mixture of a sugar syrup and fruit purée or other flavoring. But, instead of being churned in an ice-cream machine, a granita is poured into a shallow pan and frozen in a freezer. During the freezing process, the mixture must be scraped and stirred every 20 or 30 minutes so that it does not freeze solid. The resulting confection is granular, icy, and refreshing. Be aware that granita does not keep as long as sorbets or ice creams. It is best served on the day it is made, preferably within 4 hours of freezing, for the best texture.

SHERBET

Similar to sorbet, sherbet is made with fruit or fruit juice, but it may also contain milk, or in some cases egg whites and gelatin. Sherbet tends to be coarser in texture than ice cream, with a slightly tarter flavor. The result is a flavor and consistency midway between that of sorbet and ice cream.

SUGAR SYRUPS

An essential ingredient in sorbets and granitas, sugar syrup is often called "simple syrup" by cooks and chefs because it's just that: the most basic syrup. While the proportions can change, most sugar syrups are made with a 1:1 ratio of granulated sugar to water. Some are sweeter, with a 1.5:1 or even 2:1 ratio of sugar to water.

You may want to make a sugar syrup sweeter or less sweet, depending on the sweetness of the fruit you are using. Unless the fruit is especially sweet, follow the instructions included with the recipes in this book at least once before experimenting. Too much sugar will inhibit freezing.

To make a sugar syrup, cook the sugar and water in a saucepan set over medium-high heat. As the water comes to a boil, stir occasionally with a wooden spoon to encourage the sugar to melt. Even if you don't stir it, the sugar will quickly dissolve in the water and the syrup will turn clear. At this point, the syrup is ready. Once cool, the syrup should be stored in a lidded glass jar and can be refrigerated for up to 1 month.

FREEZING

When making any icy dessert in an ice-cream maker, the machine incorporates air into the ingredients as they freeze. It is this amount of air that defines the texture of the finished product. If no air is incorporated, the chilled liquid will freeze into a solid block; if too much air is incorporated, the ice cream, sorbet, or sherbet will be light and lack full flavor.

The ice-cream makers made for today's home kitchens perform beautifully and the results have a lovely consistency. If you like, you can serve ice creams, sorbets, and sherbets directly from the ice-cream machine; they will be the consistency of soft custard or soft ice cream. But for a more familiar thick, solid consistency, transfer them to another container and place in the freezer for at least 3 hours or up to 3 days.

Following are a few more tips to keep in mind when making ice cream at home:

Expect the ice-cream base to taste sweeter than the frozen ice cream. Flavor diminishes when food is cold.

If you are using an ice-cream machine that requires ice, crushing the ice first will increase its surface area. In doing so, the cold from the ice will transfer more efficiently to the ice-cream base.

Take care when adding wine or spirits of any kind to ice-cream bases. Alcohol lowers the freezing point, and too much alcohol will prevent the ice cream from setting properly.

ICE CREAM TOPPINGS

A dish of ice cream is delicious all on its own, but adding a sweet sauce or garnish makes for an irresistible treat.

CHOCOLATE SAUCE

¾ cup (6 oz/185 g) unsalted butter, cut into pieces

2 oz (60 g) unsweetened chocolate, coarsely chopped

¼ cup (¾ oz/20 g) unsweetened cocoa powder

1 cup (8 oz/250 g) sugar

Pinch of salt

1 cup (8 fl oz/250 ml) heavy (double) cream

1 teaspoon vanilla extract (essence)

In the top pan of a double boiler (page 114) set over gently simmering water, melt the butter and chocolate, stirring until smooth.

In a small bowl, stir together the cocoa, sugar, and salt. Add to the chocolate and stir to combine. Add the cream, raise the heat to medium-high, and bring to a boil over rapidly simmering water, stirring to blend. Remove from the heat, let the sauce cool for a few minutes, and then stir in the vanilla. Let the sauce cool until warm or room temperature before serving.

Use immediately, or cover and refrigerate for up to 3 days. Reheat gently over low heat. Makes about 2 cups (16 fl oz/500 ml).

HARDENING HOT FUDGE SAUCE

2 oz (60 g) unsweetened chocolate, coarsely chopped

2 tablespoons unsalted butter, cut into pieces

½ cup (4 fl oz/125 ml) water

1 cup (8 oz/250 g) plus 2 tablespoons sugar

2 tablespoons light corn syrup

2 teaspoons vanilla extract (essence)

In a heavy 1.5- to 2-qt (1.5- to 2-l) saucepan, combine the chocolate, butter, and water. Cook over medium-low heat, stirring constantly, until the chocolate melts and the sauce is smooth.

Stir in the sugar and corn syrup. Cook over medium heat, stirring frequently, until the sauce comes to a full boil. Reduce the heat to low, cover, and cook without stirring to dissolve any sugar crystals, about 2 minutes.

Uncover the pan, raise the heat to medium-low, and let the sauce boil for 5 full minutes without stirring. Remove from the heat, let the sauce cool for a few minutes, and then stir in the vanilla. Use immediately, as the sauce thickens when it cools and loses its hardening properties. The hot sauce will turn thick, chewy, and candylike when it comes in contact with cold ice cream.

The sauce can be covered and refrigerated for up to 3 days. To reheat, set a heatproof bowl or pan holding the sauce over a saucepan partially filled with gently simmering water. Stir until the sauce is hot. Makes about 1¼ cups (10 fl oz/310 ml).

BUTTERSCOTCH SAUCE

1 cup (8 oz/250 g) sugar

1 cup (8 fl oz/250 ml) light corn syrup

½ cup (4 fl oz/125 ml) heavy (double) cream

3 tablespoons unsalted butter, cut into pieces

2 tablespoons Scotch whisky (optional)

In a heavy 2- to 2.5-qt (2- to 2.5 l) saucepan over medium-high heat, cook the sugar until it turns amber, 6–8 minutes. Stir the sugar with a long-handled wooden spoon during the first 1–2 minutes of cooking; do not stir after this point and, instead, tip the pan to ensure even cooking. Do not allow the sugar to burn. If the sugar burns, turns very dark, and smells acrid, discard it and start again.

Add the corn syrup and cook until blended, stirring only as necessary. Exercise great caution, as the sugar is very hot. Use a long-handled wooden spoon and heavy pot holders to protect your hands.

Remove from the heat and very carefully pour the cream into the hot syrup. Add the butter and stir until the butter melts, the cream is thoroughly incorporated, and the sauce is smooth. Stir in the whisky, if using. Serve warm or at room temperature.

The sauce can be covered and refrigerated for up to 3 days. Reheat gently over medium heat. Makes about 2 cups (16 fl oz/500 ml).

CARAMEL SAUCE

¾ cup (6 oz/185 g) sugar

2 tablespoons water

½ teaspoon fresh lemon juice

¾ cup (6 fl oz/180 ml) heavy (double) cream

In a heavy 2- to 2.5-qt (2- to 2.5 l) saucepan, combine the sugar, water, and lemon juice. Cook over medium-high heat until it turns amber, 6–8 minutes. Stir the sugar with a wooden spoon during the first 1–2 minutes of cooking; do not stir after this point and, instead, tip the pan to ensure even cooking. Do not allow the sugar to burn. If the sugar burns, turns very dark, and smells acrid, discard it and start again.

Remove from the heat and very carefully pour the cream into the hot syrup. Take care it does not splash; the syrup is very hot. Use heavy pot holders to protect your hands and arms. Stir with a long-handled wooden spoon until the sauce is smooth and blended. Let the sauce cool to warm or room temperature. Use immediately, or cover and refrigerate for up to 3 days.

To reheat, set the bowl or pan holding the sauce over a saucepan partially filled with gently simmering water. Stir until the sauce is warm. Makes about 1 cup (8 fl oz/250 ml).

RASPBERRY SAUCE

4 cups (1¼ lb/630 g) frozen raspberries in light syrup (two 10-oz/315-g bags)

4 teaspoons arrowroot

1 tablespoon sugar or 1 tablespoon orange-flavored liqueur such as Cointreau or Grand Marnier

Put the raspberries in a sieve set over a bowl. Let thaw at room temperature until the juices are liquid, but the berries are still partially frozen. Reserve 1 cup (8 fl oz/250 ml) of the juice and transfer the berries to a another bowl.

Put the arrowroot in a small cup and slowly stir in about 1 tablespoon of the raspberry juice until smooth. Pour the remaining juice into a small saucepan and stir in the arrow-root mixture and sugar (if using the liqueur, do not add it now). Heat over medium heat, stirring, until the syrup comes to a boil. Immediately remove from the heat; do not let it boil for more than 15 or 20 seconds. Add the liqueur, if using. Pour the syrup over the berries and stir to combine. Transfer to a blender or a food processor and pulse to purée. Strain the sauce through a fine-mesh sieve into a stainless-steel bowl.

Cover and refrigerate until chilled, at least 2 hours or up to 2 days. Makes about 2 cups (16 fl oz/500 ml).

Variation Tips: For a chunky sauce, omit blending in a blender or food processor. Instead, pour the syrup over the berries as directed and stir gently to mix without crushing too many berries. To make strawberry sauce, substitute frozen strawberries in light syrup for the raspberries.

CANDIED LEMON ZEST

3 large, thick-skinned lemons

⅔ cup (5 fl oz/160 ml) water

1 cup (8 oz/250 g) sugar, plus 1 tablespoon

Use a citrus zester to remove the zest from the lemons in long strips. In a saucepan, combine the lemon zest and enough water to cover by several inches. Bring to a boil over medium-high heat and cook for 5 minutes. Drain and rinse under cold water.

Squeeze 1 or 2 of the lemons to make ⅓ cup (3 fl oz/80 ml) lemon juice. Strain the lemon juice through a fine mesh sieve to remove any seeds or pulp. Set aside. Reserve the remaining lemons for another use.

In a small, heavy saucepan, combine the water, the 1 cup (8 oz/250 g) sugar, and the reserved lemon juice. Cook over medium heat, stirring occasionally, until the sugar is dissolved, about 1 minute. Add the lemon zest and bring to a boil over medium-high heat. Reduce the heat to medium and simmer for 10 minutes. Remove the pan from the heat and let the zest and syrup cool to room temperature.

Drain the zest and reserve the syrup for another use. Put the zest in a shallow bowl. Sprinkle with the 1 tablespoon sugar and toss to coat. Let stand at room temperature to allow the zest to absorb the sugar, about 2 hours. Slide the zest onto a chopping board and chop finely. Use at once, or transfer to a covered container and refrigerate for up to 1 day. Makes about ¼ cup (1 oz/30 g).

Note: You may substitute other citrus fruit, such as grapefruit, oranges, or limes, for the lemons in this recipe.

GLOSSARY

ARROWROOT A fine, powdery starch, this thickener ground from the root of a West Indian plant is often used in place of cornstarch (cornflour) or flour in recipes for puddings and sauces. Arrowroot does not have the chalky taste of undercooked cornstarch, and it gives sauces a lovely sheen.

COCOA POWDER This powder is made by removing nearly all the cocoa butter from chocolate liquor and then grinding it to an unsweetened powder. Alkalized, or Dutch-processed, cocoa powder is milder and more soluble than nonalkalized. Nonalkalized or natural cocoa powder is slightly lighter in color but has more intense chocolate flavor than alkalized. Use the variety specified in the recipe.

CORN SYRUP Made from cornstarch, corn syrup is used to sweeten everything from commercial candies and jams to the homemade ice cream sauces in this book. It is easier to cook with than sugar syrup, as it will not crystallize when heated. Use light corn syrup for the recipes in this book; dark corn syrup will add too much flavor.

CREAM, HEAVY The key element from which ice cream derives its name, heavy cream has the most milk fat and the richest flavor. It contains between 36 and 40 percent fat. Heavy cream is also called double cream in Britain, and it may also be labeled heavy whipping cream or just whipping cream in the United States. Do not substitute light cream or half-and-half (half cream) for the heavy cream called for in the recipes in this book.

DOUBLE BOILERS A double boiler is a set of two pans, one nested atop the other with room for water to simmer in the pan below. Delicate foods such as chocolate and custards are placed in the top pan to heat them gently, or to melt them in the case of chocolate. The top pan should not touch the water beneath it, and the water is not meant to boil. A tight fit between the pans ensures that no water or steam can escape and mix with the ingredients in the top, which can cause melting chocolate to seize or stiffen.

You can create your own double boiler by placing a heatproof mixing bowl or a slightly smaller saucepan over a larger one, although it may not be as steady or the fit as tight.

EGG, RAW Eggs are sometimes used raw in meringues and other preparations. Raw eggs run a risk of being infected with salmonella or other bacteria, which can lead to food poisoning. This risk is of most concern to small children, older people, pregnant women, and anyone with a compromised immune system. If you have health and safety concerns, do not consume raw egg.

EGGS, SEPARATING Eggs are easier to separate when they are cold. Carefully crack each egg and use an egg separator to separate the white from the yolk, if you have one. (An egg separator is a small, bowl-shaped device with a center depression made to hold the yolk while the egg white slides through slots on the side into a waiting bowl.) Otherwise, hold the cracked egg over a bowl and pass the yolk back and forth between the shell halves, letting the white fall into the bowl. Drop the yolk into a separate bowl, and transfer the white to a third bowl. Separate each additional egg over an empty bowl, for if a speck of yolk gets into the whites, the whites will not whip up properly. If a yolk breaks, start fresh with another egg.

Many of the custard-based ice creams in this cookbook call for egg yolks only. If you want to store the whites for another use, keep them in a tightly lidded glass or plastic container in the refrigerator for up to 5 days or in the freezer for several months. Let the separated egg whites come to room temperature before using them in a recipe. Some ideas for recipes that call for egg whites include meringue (page 105), angel food cake, or egg-white omelets.

MILK, WHOLE An essential ingredient in many ice cream recipes, whole milk contains around 3.5 percent fat. The rich flavor of whole milk comes from its emulsified fats, its distinctive white color derives from casein protein, and its faintly sweet flavor reveals the presence of lactose, a type of sugar found only in milk. Most processed milk is fortified with vitamin D, which helps the body absorb calcium, and vitamin A. Almost all milk sold today is homogenized, which means that it has been forced through tiny holes to break its fat globules into small particles that will remain suspended evenly throughout the milk. If not homogenized, whole milk will have a layer of cream on top. Do not substitute low-fat or nonfat milk for the whole milk called for in the recipes in this book.

NONALUMINUM Selecting a cookware made from a nonreactive material such as stainless steel, enamel, or glass is important when cooking with acidic ingredients such as citrus juice or when cooking eggs. Cookware made with materials such as aluminum (and, to a lesser degree, cast iron or unlined copper) will react with acidic ingredients and the hydrogen sulfide in eggs and will impart a metallic taste and grayish color.

NUTMEG The oval, brown seed of a soft fruit, nutmeg has a warm, sweet, spicy flavor. Inside the fruit, the nutmeg seed is enclosed in a lacy red cage that, when lifted away and ground, is known as the spice mace. Whole nutmeg keeps its flavor much longer than ground nutmeg. Always grate nutmeg just before using. Use the finest rasps on a handheld grater, or a specialized nutmeg grater.

NUTS
Below are some nuts commonly used in ice creams. Since nuts contain high amounts of oil, they will eventually turn rancid. Check them for freshness before adding to a recipe.

Hazelnuts: Also known as filberts, grape-sized hazelnuts have hard shells that come to a point like an acorn, cream-colored flesh, and a sweet, rich, buttery flavor. Difficult to crack, they are usually sold already shelled.

Pecans: Native to North America, the pecan has two deeply crinkled lobes of nutmeat, much like its relative the walnut. The nuts have smooth, brown, oval shells that break easily. Their flavor is sweeter and more delicate than walnuts.

Pistachios: Pistachios have creamy tan, thin, hard, rounded outer shells. As the nuts ripen, their shells crack to reveal light green kernels.

Walnuts: The furrowed, double-lobed nutmeat of the walnut has an assertive, rich flavor. The most common variety is the English walnut, also known as the Persian walnut, which has a light brown shell that cracks easily. Black walnuts have a stronger flavor and extremely hard shells but are a challenge to find.

SALT, ROCK Mined from salt deposits rather than being processed by evaporation, rock salt has less taste than other salts and is primarily used in making ice cream in hand-cranked ice-cream makers. Because salt lowers the freezing point of water, rock salt helps to make the melting ice cold enough to freeze the ice cream.

VANILLA EXTRACT Also known as vanilla essence, this distillation lends perfume, depth, and nuance to many recipes. Avoid imitation vanilla, which is artificially flavored and has an inferior taste. Vanilla extract is most commonly made from Bourbon-Madagascar beans, and the best-quality vanilla extracts should state this on their label. For information on whole vanilla beans, see page 10.

ZEST The zest is the thin, colored portion of a citrus rind. Choose organic fruit for any recipe calling for zest, then be sure to scrub the fruit well to eliminate any residue or wax. You can use a zester, a tool designed for removing the zest in long, narrow strips, which can then be left whole or chopped. Take care to remove only the colored portion of the rind, leaving behind all of the bitter white pith.

INDEX

SIMON & SCHUSTER SOURCE
A Division of Simon & Schuster, Inc.
1230 Avenue of the Americas
New York, NY 10020

WILLIAMS-SONOMA
Founder and Vice-Chairman: Chuck Williams

WELDON OWEN INC.
Chief Executive Officer: John Owen
President: Terry Newell
Chief Operating Officer: Larry Partington
Vice President, International Sales: Stuart Laurence
Creative Director: Gaye Allen
Series Editor: Sarah Putman Clegg
Editor: Heather Belt
Designer: Teri Gardiner
Production: Chris Hemesath and Teri Bell
Production Assistant: Libby Temple

Weldon Owen wishes to thank the following
people for their generous assistance and support in
producing this book: Copy Editor Carolyn Miller;
Consulting Editors Sharon Silva and Judith Dunham;
Food Stylist Sandra Cook; Photographer's Assistants
Noriko Akiyama and Heidi Ladendorf; Assistant Food
Stylist Elisabet der Nederlanden; Proofreaders
Carrie Bradley and Desne Ahlers; Indexer Ken DellaPenta,
and Recipe Testers Carole Harlam, Peter Goodbody,
and Deborah Callan.

Set in Trajan, Utopia, and Vectora.

Williams-Sonoma Collection *Ice Cream* was
conceived and produced by Weldon Owen Inc.,
814 Montgomery Street, San Francisco,
California 94133, in collaboration with
Williams-Sonoma, 3250 Van Ness Avenue,
San Francisco, California 94109.

A Weldon Owen Production
Copyright © 2003 by Weldon Owen Inc. and
Williams-Sonoma Inc.

For information about special discounts for bulk
purchases, please contact Simon & Schuster
Special Sales: 1-800-456-6798 or
business@simonandschuster.com

Color separations by Bright Arts Graphics
Singapore (Pte.) Ltd.
Printed and bound in Singapore by Tien Wah
Press (Pte.) Ltd.

First printed in 2003.

10 9 8 7 6 5 4 3 2 1

Library of Congress Cataloging-in-Publication
Data is available.

ISBN 0-7432-4367-6

A NOTE ON WEIGHTS AND MEASURES

All recipes include customary U.S. and metric measurements. Metric conversions are based on
a standard developed for these books and have been rounded off. Actual weights may vary.